PROCLAMATION:

Aids for Interpreting the Lessons of the Church Year

HOLY WEEK

SERIES A

Krister Stendahl

FORTRESS PRESS

Philadelphia, Pennsylvania

Library of Congress Catalog Card Number 74-76926

ISBN 0-8006-4064-0

Second printing 1977
Third printing 1978

7075A78 Printed in the United States of America 1-4064

General Preface

Proclamation: Aids for Interpreting the Lessons of the Church Year is a series of twenty-six books designed to help clergymen carry out their preaching ministry. It offers exegetical interpretations of the lessons for each Sunday and many of the festivals of the church year, plus homiletical ideas and insights.

The basic thrust of the series is ecumenical. In recent years the Episcopal church, the Roman Catholic church, the United Church of Christ, the Christian Church (Disciples of Christ), the United Methodist Church, the Lutheran and Presbyterian churches, and also the Consultation on Church Union have adopted lectionaries that are based on a common three-year system of lessons for the Sundays and festivals of the church year. *Proclamation* grows out of this development, and authors have been chosen from all of these traditions. Some of the contributors are parish pastors; others are teachers, both of biblical interpretation and of homiletics. Ecumenical interchange has been encouraged by putting two persons from different traditions to work on a single volume, one with the primary responsibility for exegesis and the other for homiletical interpretation.

Despite the high percentage of agreement between the traditions, both in the festivals that are celebrated and the lessons that are appointed to be read on a given day, there are still areas of divergence. Frequently the authors of individual volumes have tried to take into account the various textual traditions, but in some cases this has proved to be impossible; in such cases we have felt constrained to limit the material to the Lutheran readings.

The preacher who is looking for "canned sermons" in these books will be disappointed. These books are one step removed from the pulpit: they explain what the lessons are saying and suggest ways of relating this biblical message to the contemporary situation. As such they are springboards for creative thought as well as for faithful proclamation of the word.

Krister Stendahl is Dean and John Lord O'Brian Professor of Divinity at the Divinity School of Harvard University. A native of Sweden, he was formerly Docent in New Testament at the University of Uppsala. The author of *The School of St. Matthew* (2nd edition; Philadelphia: Fortress Press, 1968), he is a clergyman of the Lutheran Church in America. Dean Stendahl's contribution to *Proclamation* is unique in several respects: he is himself the author of both the exegetical and the homiletical sections of this book; he has consistently treated the Gospel for the Day as the first lesson; and, his volume includes a general presentation of Matthew's view of the events of Holy Week, this view being the basis for the common lectionaries of Series A.

Table of Contents

Introduction

On the Responsibility of Preaching in Holy Week

Martin Luther often stressed that the art of responsible preaching consisted of rightly dividing Law and Gospel. In his own powerful attempts at such preaching he was eager to stress that such a division was not achieved by calling the OT Law and the NT Gospel. After all, his spiritual breakthrough and liberation happened in his studies of the Psalms.

Or we could express this principle of his by saying that responsible preaching—and Bible reading—cannot be achieved by painting Judaism, its piety and leaders, in ever more ugly and unsympathetic colors, as if the glory of Christianity would thereby shine the brighter—as if the glory and light of Jesus Christ needed such contrast to be perceived! Insecure faith falls for the temptation of seeking assurance by caricaturing the faith of others. Such a method is not a sign of faith and conviction, but of human frailty.

We must remember that, especially when we enter into Holy Week. For, as our Jewish friends can tell us in no uncertain terms, it was during the celebration of Holy Week that the worst of the pogroms were unleashed and Christians felt that they had divine sanction for their ugly paroxysms of antisemitism. We may feel above and beyond such hateful events, but we must ask ourselves why it is that in our minds—as in the Oberammergau plays—the pictures of Judas and the high priests look more Jewish than does that of Jesus. It may well have been just the opposite. We must uproot every possible plant of antisemitism from our celebration of Holy Week. If we were to add up the suffering and hatred and ridiculing jokes and habits of thoughtless thinking that Christians have piled up on the Jews over the ages—finding a sanction for it all in the passion narratives of their gospel, i.e., "good news"—then it would be a Passion Story far uglier than that of the Christian Holy Week. For that reason alone—and in the name of simple truth—our celebration of Holy Week must be one of repentance. In your preparation for Holy Week you could seek out the local rabbi and ask him to help you. Let him listen to your thoughts and tell you what he hears. For we are responsible for what people hear us say, not for what we think we are saying. And, after all, also for us this is Passover. In the early church the celebration was called by that name (*pascha*).

In our exegesis and homiletical notes I have chosen to stress what is peculiar to the different Gospels, in this Series A, especially Matthew and John. I have done so since I believe in the value of preaching "on the text" as it is given. Each of the Gospels tells the story differently. We can, of course, try to put together a harmonized or composite picture of what might actually have happened. That is guesswork and the field of clever historians. It is an important and interesting task. But as a preacher I prefer to be guided by the texts as they are given to us. Thus I like to learn how a Matthew or a John saw and witnessed, and I like to be helped to specificity and clarity in my sermons and my grasp of the mysteries by learning from them what to see, and how to see, and how to witness to the words and acts of Jesus and of those around Jesus. Let us remember that each of the Gospels was once the full and only Gospel for the church where it took shape and was read.

But if we were to go behind the sources toward what actually might have happened when Jesus was executed in Jerusalem, what would we learn? That question is important, especially in our repentance of anti-semitism. For as the story grew and developed, the burden of guilt was shifted from Pilate to the high priests, from the high priests to the Pharisees, and on to "the Jews." The mystery of him "who came to his own, and his own received him not" became secularized.

I have quoted this phrase from John 1:11 as the KJV translates the Greek literally; it is interesting to note that the RSV translates "he came to his own home, and his own people received him not." That is a "correct" translation—sort of. No doubt John had in mind the rejection of Jesus by what he calls "the Jews," i.e., the Jewish authorities. But by adding such specificity the RSV locks the word into a perpetual pattern of anti-judaism, and makes it more difficult for the reader to feel the wider and deeper meaning of what John also sees as a universal pattern of human reaction to God's gracious gifts. The NEB has felt the problem in such translations or interpretations, and renders the Greek as "He entered his own realm, and his own would not receive him." That "realm" is not only his Jewish matrix and people. That realm is the whole creation, the world "that owed its being to him" (v. 10).

The glory of how the gospel became the joy of gentiles became celebrated by anti-Jewish rhetoric, and Paul had little hearing for his sharp warning to his gentile converts: When you think of the Jews, don't be proud, but stand in awe! (Rom. 11:20). And when that pride of a small and grateful and beleaguered Christian minority became coupled with majority status and power, then the use of the Jews as the scapegoat became truly satanic. In the mystery of Christ's passion there is no need for finding a scapegoat. He and he alone is our scapegoat: the Lamb of God that carries the sins of us all out of the world (cf. John 1:29).

There is a growing consensus among biblical historians as to the historical events of Holy Week [see, e.g., the clear and useful study by William R. Wilson, *The Execution of Jesus.* Scribners Paperback (SL 401), 1970]. Jesus was executed by the Roman authorities; hence he was crucified, not stoned (cf. Stephen, Acts 6-7). He was put to death as a potential or actual political troublemaker. The role of the Jewish authorities in Jerusalem—who had little popular support in those days, as they tried to preserve as best they could the limited freedom of Judea under Roman occupation—is not easy to assess. It seems reasonable that they saw the popularity of Jesus and his messianic sounding claims as a threat to the delicate balance of political order in the land, and that they felt as worried about his activities as about those of the zealots. Thus they followed the principle of all legislatures and administrators through the ages: "It is better that one person dies for the people, lest the whole nation be destroyed" (John 11:51).

There can be no doubt that Jesus was executed as a revolutionary, i.e., for political reasons. It seems obvious to most Christians that he was not, that "his kingdom was not of this world," and that his message was a spiritual one, as we say. But such a distinction has never worked in the history of this world. It is not a question of whether the revolution comes with sword or with words of insight. The authorities are smarter than that. They know enough to fear words and ideas. The early Christian martyrs were not put to death for their faith, but as subversives. Luther was not banned for his doctrines, but for threatening the order of the empire. The Berrigans were not imprisoned for their faith, but for threatening the authority of the state when they turned over the tables in the temples of military patriotism in a symbolic yet devastating act—like Jesus once in Jerusalem.

Perhaps it is part of the incarnation that there can be no comfortable distinction between the spiritual and political. In Holy Week we celebrate the ultimate political punishment—the crucifixion—of the Spirit incarnate, Jesus Christ.

The two Gospels which will occupy us this Holy Week are the ones least suited for the telling of the story in human terms. I shall try to show how their reflection on the mystery of Christ's death has led them away from the perspectives of human tragedy, or a martyrdom to be emulated by the followers of Jesus. The primary "actor" in their drama is none other than God himself. Matthew and John express that obvious yet difficult fact in different ways. In the Johannine encounter between Jesus and Pilate the style is that of irony, for only in irony can the magnitude of this event be fitted into human events and conversations (cf. below, on 1 Cor. 1:18-25, pp. 33-34).

Which all finally leads us to remember that the observance of Holy Week is not the original form under which the Christians remembered and were reminded of the events surrounding Jesus' death. Perhaps it was not until the later centuries with their Christian pilgrimages to Jerusalem (beginning in the 4th century) and with the stations on the way to the cross, the *via dolorosa,* that one began to follow the events stage by stage. Such a practice and such a tradition of meditation and reflection tended to draw the attention to the feelings and attitudes not only of Jesus, but also of the other actors, silent or vociferous. In such a tradition of meditation and preaching we find how in many ways there is a denying Peter and a betraying Judas and a wavering Pilate, etc., etc., in all of us. Such preaching is all well and good, but . . .

But Matthew and John may help us closer to an earlier and deeper perspective, where the mysterious death of Jesus Christ the Son of God absorbs our minds so fully that we almost forget the bystanders and the moral lessons, and begin to join in the oldest hymn about the cross that we have:

> Bend thy boughs, O Tree of Glory,
>   Thy relaxing sinews bend;
> For awhile the ancient rigor
>   That thy birth bestowed, suspend;

And the King of heavenly beauty
On thy bosom gently tend.

(Service Book and Hymnal of the Lutheran Church in America [1958], hymn #61. Hereinafter cited as SBH.)

Or we may sing in a very different idiom, yet, again seeing nothing but Jesus and him crucified—if by the grace of God those who gave us that song can allow us to borrow it, for it was written out of the suffering that we white Christians caused upon the black slaves:

Were you there when they crucified my Lord?
O, sometimes it causes me to tremble, tremble . . .

(SBH 500)

Holy Week

In speaking about Holy Week, we should first remember that according to the Christian way of thinking, Sunday is the first day of the week. Thus the week runs from Sunday through Saturday. In secular society today—unconsciously and sometimes consciously—it is rather Monday that is experienced as the first day. I agree with those sociologists and anthropologists who believe that the structuring of time by the rhythm of calendar and holy days is the means by which a religion influences the life of people most deeply and lastingly. Thus I find it important to reflect on "The Christian Week," that delightfully "immoral" structure that begins with the "day off."

From Israel and the Jewish community the church inherited the week with its Sabbath as the seventh day to be hallowed (Exod. 20:8-11; cf. Gen. 2:1-3), but in the early church the day of the Resurrection, which was the first day of the week (*mia tōn sabbatōn*, Mark 16:2 par.), became the magnet that pulled the Christian community together in special assembly (Acts 20:7; 1 Cor. 16:2); this became the Lord's Day (Rev. 1:10; Didache 14:1; cf. Ps. 118:24). Ignatius (ca. AD 115) writes "If then they who walked in ancient customs came to a new hope, no longer living for the Sabbath, but for the Lord's Day, on which also our life sprang up through him and his death . . ." (Letter to the Magnesians 9:1).

This new center of gravity in the Christian church came to change the structure of the week as time went on. In the beginning the Saturday sabbath was kept in Jewish milieus, and in gentile settings the Christians had no power to ask for a day of rest. But when the Christian communities grew in numbers and influence in the gentile world, the observance of the sabbath as the day of rest, and as the day set aside to be hallowed, became attached to Sunday rather than Saturday. The Christian week came to begin on the note of the celebration of life and of the sabbath rest. (See further Willy Rordorf, *Sunday: The History of the Day of Rest and Worship in the Earliest Centuries of the Christian Church*

[1969], and Harald Riesenfeld, "The Sabbath and the Lord's Day in Judaism, the Preaching of Jesus and Early Christianity," in *The Gospel Tradition* [1969], pp. 111-137.)

I find that arrangement beautiful and full of meaning, as have Christian thinkers through the ages. It is a symbol incarnated in the very rhythm of our most common experiences. We do not work a long week in order to get to the Sabbath. We begin in the sign and mood and celebration of the new creation, the resurrection. The first day is also what Jewish apocalyptic dreams referred to as the "Eighth Day," the beginning of the new creation.

As we enter Holy Week through the gate of the Sunday of the Passion, and through the gates of Jerusalem, the structure of that week impresses on us that Easter Day is another story, and belongs to "next week." The texts of Passion Sunday with the overwhelmingly long reading of the Matthean account of Jesus' last days are given in order that we lose ourselves in that drama and the uncertainties of the outcome as it actually must have looked and felt to the followers of Jesus—and perhaps to Jesus himself.

The Sunday of the Passion, Palm Sunday

Lutheran	*Roman Catholic*	*Episcopal*	*Pres./UCC/Chr.*	*Methodist/COCU*
Isa. 50:4-9*a*	Isa. 50:4-7	Zech. 9:9-12	Isa. 50:4-7	Isa. 50:4-9a
Phil. 2:5-11	Phil. 2:6-11	Phil. 2:5-11	Phil. 2:5-11	Phil. 2:5-11
Matt. 26:1-27:66 (long), or Matt. 27:11-54 (short)	Matt. 26:14-27:66 (long), or Matt. 27:11-54 (short)	Matt. 26:36-27:54	Matt. 21:1-11	Matt. 26:14-27:66

This year the Gospel for the Sunday of Holy Week is the Matthean passion narrative; in other years it will be Mark and Luke that guide us into the events and mysteries of Christ's passion. And John will be our guide each Good Friday. With such an emphasis for this Sunday, the old designation "Passion Sunday" has been moved from the fifth Sunday in Lent to this day, the first day of Holy Week. The fifth Sunday in Lent now gives us a foretaste of Jesus' powers of life and resurrection (John 11)—so that we do not lose heart in the dire events of Holy Week.

With such a shift in emphasis, many will miss the note and texts of Palm Sunday, with the modest, yet triumphant entry of Jesus into the city of Jerusalem. It is therefore important to follow the suggestion (*The Church Year: Calendar and Lectionary,* Inter-Lutheran Commission on Worship [1973], p. 74) that the service on the Sunday of the Passion begin with a procession and distribution of branches (according to the flora of your location, palms in the south, pussy willows in the north, etc.), and with the reading of Matt. 21:1-11.

The rubrics say that this gospel text "may be substituted for the Gospel for the Day." I would think, however, that it would be more helpful, both ecumenically, and for the richest edification of the congregation, if we did read the Matthean Passion (chaps. 26-27) as the Gospel for the Day. Due to the length of the text, the congregation should remain seated, even if the shorter form (27:11-54) is used. For this kind of gospel reading is different in form and function from most gospel readings. We pay best homage and attention by listening in a mood of quiet meditation, and so let the magnitude of the events sink into our conscious and unconscious being. The very length of the reading gives a special character to the day. It may appear "too long" at first, but once we have settled down and are listening, we recognize that the events are woven together in such a manner that they deserve to impress and act upon us in their fullness.

This is one reading that must be done by someone who reads well and with a sense for the meaning of the text. While that is not always the pastor, neither should this be an occasion for lay participation for its own sake. I also have reservations about the wisdom of the rubrics (p. 75) when they suggest a "play reading" format. I believe the guiding principle should be quality of reading rather than method, and the quality should be measured by its being conducive to meditation and reflection. The drama of the Passion is most impressive when presented quietly, without rhetoric or dramatics.

It is obvious that the sermon on this day should be short, lifting up a word, a thought, a theme. It would be proper to take one's lead from the gospel of the procession with palms (Matt. 21:1-11) as it was read in the entrance rite. It may be that such a balance in the service would be quite good: Let the majestic account of the full Matthean Passion be given for private meditation; and then lift up the entry into the week and into the city of confrontation. Whether we follow such a suggestion or not, this year the accent and the perspective should be consciously Matthean.

The Text for the Palm Sunday Procession: Matt. 21:1-11—Exegesis. This reading includes a reaction of the people in Jerusalem to Jesus' entry (vv. 10-11; cf. however, John 12:12-13. See below p. 29) which is found only in Matthew. Matthew uses strong language in describing the impact of Jesus' entry, but the NEB's "the whole city went wild with excitement" is not the right way to catch the import of Matthew's "the whole city was shaken." The point is not "excitement," but rather the momentous coming of the Messiah, for Matthew uses that same word for the earthquake at Jesus' death (27:51), and for the shaken guards at the tomb (28:4). He thereby points to the manifestation of divine and cosmic power, not to psychological excitement. In more learned language: the coming of Jesus into the city is a christophany. According to Matthew the people at large see Jesus as a prophet (cf. 21:46), whereas to him Jesus is more than a prophet (cf. 16:14-15).

In Jewish liturgies of the time the word "hosanna" (Ps. 118:25: "Save us!", the same Hebrew root as in the name "Jesus") had lost its original meaning as a cry for salvation, and had become an expression of praise: "Hosanna to the Son of David" (so only Matthew); Luke interprets the hosanna by the words: "Peace in heaven and glory in the highest" (19: 38; cf. the song of the angels in Luke 2:14).

One of the striking features of Matthew is his typical reference to the fulfillment of an OT prophecy introduced by a so-called formula quotation (v. 4). His quotation (Zech. 9:9, introduced by a phrase from Isa. 62:11; cf. John 12:15), is the more interesting since Matthew finds special meaning in the reference to both a donkey and a colt (this from Mark's reference to a colt on whom no one had sat, hence its mother must have been there too). Thus the scriptures were fulfilled with much precision. That fulfillment is more important to Matthew than are realism and practicality: "and he sat upon *them.*"

The Matthean account is more concise than Mark's. Matthew's Jesus is a forceful figure: what he says happens. Hence Matthew does not need Mark's follow-up report that the two disciples found it to be just as Jesus said (Mark 11:4-6). Of course they did!

Jesus stages this entry into Jerusalem. He now goes public, but Matthew's quotation makes it clear that the image is one of power coupled with the anti-hero image of humility; the king is the promised king, but the promise is in conscious contrast to the image of the legions and the horses of the Romans. Yet he is not docile. In Matthew this is especially striking since the entry is immediately followed by the cleansing of the temple (not so in Mark and Luke).

Matt. 21:1-11—Homiletical Notes. Sermons often stress the tragic and revealing contrast between the homage at Jesus' entry and the cry for crucifixion a few days later. I doubt that Matthew saw it that way. He is much more interested in the majesty of Jesus than in the psychology of followers and opponents. Perhaps we should follow his lead. Jesus comes to challenge the world of the political and religious establishment. Between the entry and the passion lie the five chapters of confrontation (chaps. 21-25). He entered Jerusalem in a demonstration—without a permit. He "borrowed" the donkey and the colt without asking permission. His followers showed no regard for property as they took branches and were careless with their clothes. Here is a special occasion, exuberance without prudence. Here is celebration.

Before the passion comes the jubilation. And in a way, it is only for those that are that taken by Jesus that the passion makes sense. In Matthew we have a royal passion, a cosmic drama and mystery.

This same Gospel also belongs—as an alternative—to the First Sunday in Advent (Series A): Christ comes to his church at the beginning of the church year. Then the passion is far off, and the emphasis may be on the cleansing of the temple that follows immediately in the Matthean account. But on Palm Sunday the passion casts its deep shadow:

> Ride on, ride on in majesty!
> In lowly pomp ride on to die!
> (SBH 73)

Or, as it says in Ps. 45:4: "In your majesty ride forth victoriously for the cause of truth and the meekness of justice."

The Matthean Gospel for Passion Sunday (26:1-27:66)—Exegesis. Since Matthew is to be our guide and interpreter, we must try to get hold of his perspective: we must become clear on what is peculiar to his account. He follows Mark far more closely than does Luke or John. This can be seen from the distribution of the traditional Seven Last Words of Jesus. Mark and Matthew together have only one, *Eli, Eli, lama sabaktani,* i.e., the cry of desolation: "My God, my God, why have you forsaken me?" (Ps. 22).

Luke, as always, has the most humanly endearing words, three of them, and has not retained the Marcan cry of desolation. Rather there are: "Father, forgive them . . ." (23:34; but not found in the best manuscripts; cf. Isa. 53:12: ". . . and made intercession for the transgressors"; and Acts 7:60 where Stephen prays: "Lord, do not hold this sin against them"); the assurance of paradise to the criminal at his side (23:43); the beautiful and trusting words "Father, into your hands I commit my spirit" (23:46; cf. Ps. 31:5).

The remaining three words are found in John: "I thirst" (19:26); "Mother, see your son . . ." (19:28); "It is accomplished" (John 19:30).

These three sets of words are helpful indicators of the tones and perspectives of the various passion narratives. In Luke—as is the case throughout his Gospel, and also in Acts—there is much emphasis on the deep, loving, and trusting piety of Jesus, and of those in tune with it (Simeon, Mary, Elizabeth, Zachariah, etc., Luke 1 and 2). In his last hours, Jesus—duly strengthened by an angel (Luke 22:43; again, the text is uncertain, indicating that this motif may have developed further once it was there in Luke; cf. the Matthean function of the army of angels, 26:53)—exemplifies that unshaken love and trust.

In John the passion is victorious. Jesus' death is his "glorification" (12:23), and by his cross he is "lifted up" like the healing serpent in the wilderness (3:14; Num. 21:8; cf. John 8:28; 12:32, 34). His call "I thirst" is not an expression of human suffering and need, but is motivated by his concern for the fulfillment of scripture (19:28; cf. Ps. 69:22). The NEB gives a good interpretation when its translates: "After that, Jesus, aware that all had now come to its appointed end [*tetelestai*], said in fulfillment of Scripture, 'I thirst' . . . Having received the wine, he said, 'It is accomplished!' " [*tetelestai,* i.e., that same perfect passive]. Here the final word of Jesus is one of victory. He is not overcome—he has overcome.

It is further enlightening to keep in mind that we have a fifth account of the passion, in the non-canonical Gospel of Peter (see Appendix, pp. 55-58). Here the image of Jesus is not only majestic and victorious, but beyond pain—"as one having no pain"; and the translation of Ps. 22 (*Eli, eli* . . .) reads "My power, my power, you have left me!" Having said that, "he was taken up." The divine power, the divine element in Jesus never did die. What was divine in Jesus had just been housed in his body, and was beyond pain and destruction. Orthodox Christianity came to reject such a way of thinking and speaking, since it lacked the realism of incarnation and tended to make the faith a spiritual and unrelated side-track to the life of Jesus and in the life of the believers. But it is important to remember that the tendencies in the Johannine passion narrative—with the divine power of Jesus and his unshaken union with the Father—do point in that direction, just as, for John, the death of the individual believer is "non-important"; the only thing that really matters is the right relationship to Jesus Christ in faith: "Those who believe in me shall live even if they die, and everyone who lives and believes in me shall not die ever" (John 11:26); and "Those who hear my word and believe him who sent me have eternal life and do not come under judgment, but have passed (already) out of death into life" (John 5:24).

We have dwelt at some length on the various passion accounts. It is only by comparing them and by a grasp of their distinctive perspectives that we can properly assess what is peculiar to each, and, for our purpose, what is peculiar to Matthew.

We began by saying that Matthew follows Mark more closely than do the Gospels according to Luke or John (or Peter). But Matthew's telling of the passion can also be described as more akin to the Johannine than to the Lukan tendencies. In Matthew as in John we meet a Jesus who is much in command. As was his style in chap. 21 (the entry into Jerusalem), so also in 26:17-20 (the preparation for the meal), Matthew shortens the account to the effect that Jesus' orders are enough. There is no asking for the room, just the majestic: "My time is at hand [cf. John 12:23, 7:6]. In your house I will celebrate the passover with my disciples!" It is also striking how only Matthew's account begins with Jesus' own proclamation of his crucifixion (26:1-2). He also orders Judas: "Friend, do what you are here to do!" (26:50; so translates NEB correctly, as over against the harmonizing translations of the KJV, RSV, etc.: "Friend, wherefore art thou come?" cf. also John 13:27). In short, Jesus is in command, even in his passion.

He is aware of his power and his prerogatives as he moves toward the fulfillment of God's plan. He knows that he could ask God to supply him with an army of angels—but how then would the scriptures be fulfilled? (26:53 f.). This motif is considerably expanded in the Johannine dialogue between Jesus and Pilate (cf. esp. John 18:36). In Matthew it also serves as the rationale for Christian non-violence (cf. Matt. 5:38-42), as it is part of the rebuke of one of Jesus' followers who cut off the ear of the high priest's servant (26:51-54); in John it is Peter who pulls his sword (18:10), and in Luke—the compassionate, or even romantic evangelist—Jesus heals the ear of the servant (22:51).

Another special perspective in Matthew's account I would refer to as the cosmic dimension. There is the eclipse of the sun and the rending of the curtain before the Holy of Holies in the temple (as in Mark and Luke), but also an earthquake and the splitting of the rocky ground (27:51). Actually, this powerful event is not only part of the drama of death and defeat, but here on Good Friday the resurrection already begins: "And the tombs were opened and many bodies of the saints who had died were raised up, and going out of their tombs—after his resurrection—they entered the holy city and appeared to many" (NEB: "where many saw them"). Although this chronology of events did not quite fit the pattern of the *kerygma*—the formulas by which the church came to stylize its confession and its accounts of the death and resurrection of Jesus (cf. 1 Cor. 15:3 etc.)—it did survive in Matthew, helped by the harmonizing additional phrase "after his resurrection." It constitutes a significant reminder of a striking way of witnessing to the close link between the death of Jesus and the beginning of the vindication, the resurrection of all God's witnesses—martyrs—saints. This cosmic dimension of his death is even stronger in the Gospel of Peter where we read: "And then they pulled the spikes [the spikes are not mentioned in the canonical accounts, except in retrospect in John 20:25] out of the hands of the Lord and placed him on the ground [*gē*] and the whole earth [*hē gē pasa*] shook, and there was great fear. Then the sun broke through and it was found to be 3 p.m. . . ." (Gospel of Peter 21 f.).

In the Gospel of Peter the confession of the soldiers, "To be sure, he was the [or: a] son of God" (45), is prompted by the events by which the tomb is opened. In Mark this same confession is based on the manner of Jesus' death: "When the centurion . . . saw that he expired in such a manner [many manuscripts make it even more explicit, adding "with a cry"], he said: 'To be sure this man was a/the son of God'" (15:39). In Luke the confession of the centurion comes at the same place, refers to "what happened," is further underscored ("he praised God, saying . . ."), and has the form "This man was really righteous (just, innocent)." At first glance it would appear that Matthew just follows Mark here, but actually he is closer to what we saw in the Gospel of Peter; not only because the confession is given by the centurion in consort with his fellow soldiers, but also because it is motivated by their seeing "the earthquake and the things that happened, they were much awe-struck and said: 'To be sure he was a/the son of God'" (27:54). It is important that it is the cosmic event, the earthquake and the split tombs, that prompt this confession. Again, in Matthew everything tends toward theophanies and christophanies, i.e., the manifestation of God's power and kingdom. For John, see below, pp. 48-49.

The Christian image of Jesus before Pilate comes to a large extent from the Gospel of John (18:28-19:22). There Jesus and Pilate have an extensive conversation in private, as two kingdoms face each other in their representatives (18:36). In the synoptic Gospels Jesus maintains his silence also before Pilate, apart from the mysterious answer to Pilate's question whether he is the king of the Jews: *sy legeis* ("you say," Matt. 27:11). This answer is consciously ambiguous, meaning "That is what you say, but I would not use those words" and/or "You say it—and you are right." Matthew uses a similar expression (*sy eipas*) in Jesus' answer to Judas (26:25), and to the High Priest (26:64; Mark has "I am," while Luke has "You say that I am"). This answer may recapture an Aramaic idiom, but its ambiguity remains and is no doubt intended—and spelled out at length in John 18:34-38

Matthew follows Mark in that Jesus maintains his silence before Pilate, but his portrait of Pilate is further elaborated. He stresses Pilate's role as the Roman governor, a title he is fond of stressing, perhaps as the fulfillment and prototype of the apocalyptic prophecy as to the martyrdom of his followers (Matt. 10:18; cf. Mark 13:9; Luke 21:12). His Pilate has more initiative, as in the Barabbas event (Matt. 27:17; cf. Mark 15:8). But the decisive Matthean elaborations are the warning message from Pilate's wife (27:19), and his symbolic assertion of his innocence by the washing of his hands and the ensuing answer of the people: "His blood upon us and upon our children!" (The Greek sentence has no verb; 27:24-25; cf. Jer. 26:15; and Gospel of Peter 1).

Matthew's Pilate also grants the request for a guard at the tomb—with an ironic tone in his voice: "You may have your guard . . . go and make it secure as best you can" (27:65, NEB). And when the chief priests bribe that guard, they promise to "satisfy the governor and keep you out of trouble" (28:14).

Thus we can see clearly how in Matthew the simple Marcan image of Pilate—who "knew that it was out of envy [NEB: "spite"] that the chief priests had handed him over" (15:10), and who ordered the crucifixion, since it was not worth alienating them and the crowd in this case (15:15)—has grown into a conscious stress on Pilate's personal conviction that Jesus was innocent, and an even more conscious emphasis on the guilt of the Jews (see also the sharper form of the chief priests' and elders' pressure on the people, persuading them "to ask for Barabbas and to destroy Jesus" (Matt. 27:20).

Another distinct feature of the Matthean account is the elaboration of the role and fate of Judas (26:14-16, 25, 47-50; 27:3-10; see p. 35). As in John (13:21-30) there is a secret understanding between Jesus and

Judas as to the latter's grim act, an understanding hidden from the others by the mysterious words of Jesus (*sy eipas*, 26:25; *eph ho parei*, 26:50). In John, Judas is a thief (12:6; cf. 13:29; see below, p. 24), in the synoptics he is paid by the chief priests. In Matthew this payment is interpreted in the light of the scriptures (Zech. 11:12; Exod. 21:32; Jer. 32:7 ff.), and the violent death of Judas is tied to the Potter's Field and the Field of Blood (cf. Acts 1:15-20). The "secret understanding" between Jesus and Judas is another sign of how Matthew's Jesus remains in command: nothing happens that is not as it must be, and the detailed unfolding of scriptural prophecy strengthens that note as the end of Judas is surrounded by the chief priests' unwitting fulfillment of prophecy.

From Goethe to Jesus Christ Superstar there have been various attempts—with their precedents in the early history of the church—at interpreting Judas in a positive manner, e.g., as the devoted disciple who was so sure of Jesus' messianic power that, if Jesus could only be forced to show that power against his opponents, then the kingdom would come and God would vindicate his messiah. All such interpretations, however, overlook the fact that—perhaps especially in Matthew—the unfolding of the will and plan of God does not make any of the participants in the drama a puppet or just an agent. The rabbinic dictum holds: "Everything is predicted—and free will is given" (Aboth 3:19). The free will of Judas is clearly depicted as evil, and he knows it, even toward his ultimate despair in suicide. It is striking, however, that Matthew has a more tragic view of Judas than has Luke, with his reference to how Satan entered Judas (22:3), or John who agrees with Luke (13:2, 27) and in addition pictures him as an embezzler (12:6). The lack of these traits in the Matthean portrait is due to a less dualistic structure of Matthean theology. As in Judaism, and in Paul, the monotheistic impulse leads to a stronger accent on God's sovereignty also in the drama of evil. The accent is not on the conflict with evil forces, but on the mysterious yet orderly steps toward the goal set by God.

Thus the passion as told by Matthew is a powerful account of the death of Jesus in which God's will and the prophecies of the scriptures unfold with divine necessity. The roles of the participants are made quite distinct. The responsibility of the Jewish leaders is heightened, Pilate is more clearly critical of them and their motives, and the crowd is more forcefully pressured into doing their bidding. The acts of Judas are deliberate and decisive, and his gruesome role is known to Jesus and supported by him. Joseph of Arimathea, who tends to the burial of Jesus (27:57-61), is not a member of the Sanhedrin (so Mark and Luke), but is a wealthy man and a follower of Jesus (so also in John 19:38, but there "secretly, out of fear for the Jews"; cf. Nicodemus, John 3, and 19:39). Thus the line between those for and those against Jesus is more distinct. And as Jesus had entered the city on an animal on which nobody had sat before, so he now is laid in a new tomb (27:60; so also John 19:41; cf. Luke 23:53).

The lines and contours are drawn more distinctly, and the drama is made the more majestic by what we have called the stronger cosmic dimension of his death, the earthquake, the opening of the tombs, the tone of awe/fear that Matthew brings in as the setting of the confession of the soldiers at the cross: "To be sure, this man was a/the son of God."

And yet, Matthew does not go the Johannine way. His Jesus suffers, he utters the cry of despair, he retains his silence also before Pilate. Jesus' majestic *via dolorosa* remains a passion, a human drama, not a glorification.

The Matthean Passion—Homiletical Notes. To follow Jesus on his *via dolorosa* with Matthew as our guide is to experience the long hours of mounting violence and increasing agony. It is the story of an ever more lonely Jesus. His loneliness, majestic at first, becomes overshadowed by the agony, and in the cry of despair there is the tone of the ultimate loneliness, forsaken by God. Yet the drama progresses with a firm grasp of how it all serves God's will and purpose. Especially in Matthew the form of the questions raised or implicit in the drama is never "Why?" but "For what purpose?" The mood is finality, not causality, as is the case so often in the scriptures, and in the teaching of Jesus.

The acts and words—or the quietness and the silence—in the drama thus become manifestations of God's power and Christ's glory, shining through the darkness of a grim and hostile world.

For the world is grim, and evil is evil. In Matthew's passion the human and psychological interest—partly romantic, partly realistic—and the sensitivity of a Luke have been cancelled out by Matthew's sharpening of confrontation and conflict. It is only by reflection that we can recognize how the acts and decisions of the Jewish leaders and of Pilate, and the miserable record of the frightened disciples—only the women remained faithful in their love and sorrow, and only outsiders hailed him and tended to his burial—must have appeared very reasonable and even wise to them at the time.

The clarity of guilt and the strong red thread of God's purposes, as Matthew sees them both in retrospect, should never blind us to the awesome truth that when history is in the making, before it has been organized and interpreted, such things are never that clear. If that is forgotten, Christians easily read the passion story in a self-righteous mood. It becomes almost inconceivable to us how the leaders could be so evil and the governor so irresponsible.

But I can well imagine the leaders coming home to their wives late that morning, saying: "We had a very difficult case in the council. We tried to be wise and understanding, but he was impossible and totally unwilling to bend or even cooperate. So we had to . . ." And judged by high standards of political wisdom and administrative competence, both their decision and Pilate's actions would be acceptable to us—if they were not part of this story.

These were not evil people. These were not people trying to scheme or even enjoying their wicked scheming. On the contrary, they decided what they honestly considered to be best for all under the circumstances. The gruesome truth of the passion narrative is one well known from history: Most evil—serious evil—in this world is done by people who think they are doing good. Evil is not that popular. If evil were done only by those who ganged together and said: "Let us be evil together!", then evil would not spread far. No, most evil is done by people who think they are good and doing their best. . . . So the question is obvious: What am I doing now, what am I involved in now—shouting or timidly silent—that actually perpetuates innocent suffering in the world? My intentions are not to be trusted. To be of good will is not enough (cf. 1 Cor. 4:4). Paul said it well: "There is nothing surprising about that; Satan himself masquerades as an angel of light" (2 Cor. 11:14, NEB; cf. "Lucifer," Isa. 14:12). We claim to love the light, but, as John says, when light came into the world it appeared that we really did not (John 3:19).

The purposeful perspective of Matthew unmasks such self-deception. Would that we always learned from him in time! We come to think about the message of the farewell parable in Matthew where Jesus sees the despised and needy as continuing his presence in the world (25:31-46).

Also, the very death of Jesus is seen by Matthew in retrospect: the enormity of the death of God's Son, a cosmic and global drama, woven together with the vindication of all martyrs and the beginning of the general resurrection (27:51 ff.). But when it happened—as it must have looked on the human level, as it even felt in the heart and mind of Jesus, at the breaking point of his total loneliness—it was different. His last words were those of despair. Then there was a moment of silence, a moment of darkness, of nothing.

It is important that we catch that moment. For his death was real. On the human level he had been defeated. It is not true to say that such love as he had could not be overcome. It was. God had to make a new beginning—in the resurrection. And God did.

But in this world truth and justice and love—even incarnate in the wonderful Jesus of Nazareth—can be defeated and trampled down. Among us here love's labor is often lost. Evil is strong indeed.

Our hope is not a romantic optimism, the rope trick of positive thinking. Our hope is in God's power to begin again, to renew destroyed life. Even the majestic Jesus of the Gospel of Matthew died in utter loneliness, without a sign or token of life in his soul or body. But God began again. We are defeated, even the Son of God was defeated. But God was not.

The silence between Good Friday and Easter morning is the time to purify our hope from all false reasons and props. It is the moment to learn to love not the gifts of God—they can be taken away from our life and consciousness—but to love God who gives us life in his time and his way—and that abundantly. But that is Easter.

First Lesson: Isa. 50:4-9a—Exegesis. Holy Week brings before us—for obvious reasons—the four famous Songs of the Servant of Yahweh: Isa. 42:1-4 (Monday), 49:1-6 (Tuesday), 50:4-9 (Sunday and Wednesday) and 52:13–53:12 (Good Friday). These songs are not designated as special songs or units in the biblical text itself, but were identified and isolated by the scholar Bernhard Duhm in 1892, and it has become common practice to speak of them as such ever since. The first three of them do have a "response" (42:5-9, 49:7-13, 50:10-11).

The third song (50:4-9) expresses the confidence of the Servant as he faces conflict and enemies. It is a song of trust in God's help and vindication in times of ridicule and accusations. Thus it fits well as a scriptural introit to Holy Week. In the light of Near Eastern parallels, the acts mentioned in v. 6 are rather those of ridicule and insult than of physical suffering, and it should be noted that the emphasis is rather on shame (also v. 7) than on suffering, as is also the case in the famous words of Jesus concerning the taking up of one's cross (Matt. 16:24), i.e., the willingness to be ostracized from respectable society.

There is no good reason for not including v. 9b, the last words of the Song. The assurance of vindication (9a)—in the style found also in Rom. 8:31-34—is reinforced by the knowledge that the powerful are not to last; cf. Isa. 40:6, "all flesh is grass."

The "response" or the "comment of the Lord" (vv. 10-11) helps to interpret the Song rightly. It urges the followers of the Servant to trust his word and his authority even when there is no sign of his glory, and to resist the temptation of lighting their own little fires to dispel the darkness. Rather they should wait in the darkness until God's light returns and the Servant is proven right.

Isa. 50:4-9—Homiletical Notes. The secret of sustained confidence in God—especially in situations of ridicule and adversities—is the open ear. Without our listening to God's word we have nothing to say—to the weary or to anyone (v. 4).

The confidence in God and his vindication is not a static conviction or a doctrinal firmness. Strength is often described as standing pat. What is the difference between "stonewalling," and the attitude of the Servant when he has set his face "like a flint"? What is the difference between being strong in an arrogant manner, and Luther's "Here I stand."? Answer: The open ear.

Morning by morning our strength and our faith need to be given to us. The strength of the Servant and the servants of God is not something they have; not even out of the firmness of their convictions. The strength and confidence come from the quiet joy that God deigned to speak to me this morning through his word, his teaching. That is how the faith remains a living thing, a gift which I can never own, but do receive.

This world has wicked ideas about what is "strong," and also in religious matters there is often a wrong understanding of what it means to have a strong faith. The strength of faith should not be measured by the tone of certainty in our affirmations, but by our willingness to be renewed by listening, day by day. The strength is organic, the strength of a healthy heart, not the strength of stone or steel—or plastic.

Second Lesson: Phil. 2:5-11—Exegesis. In Phil. 2:6-11 we have one of the oldest Christian hymns. The vocabulary is not the one we know well from Paul's letters. There can be little doubt that Paul here uses a Christ hymn he has come across. Thus we have here a significant example of how some Christians spoke, and thought, and sang twenty to twenty-five years after the death of Jesus.

In the NT striking christological material is preserved as it was helpful for strengthening ethical admonitions (see e.g. Mark 10:45; 1 Peter 2:21-25), and in the same manner Paul brings in this hymn as part of his admonition to consider the quality and needs of others above those of oneself.

The NEB gives the two equally possible meanings of v. 5, the connecting link between the admonition and the hymn: 1) "Let your bearing towards one another arise out of your life in Christ Jesus"; or 2) "Have that bearing towards one another which was also found in Christ Jesus." An overly literal rendering of the Greek would be: "That think in you which also in Christ Jesus."

While a contemporary Bible reader may hear in this hymn many allusions to OT passages and themes (Adam, Satan, Isa. 52 and 53, etc.), none of these allusions fits the basic pattern or the terminology of the hymn. It should rather be read as a Christian song about the descent and ascent of a divine savior—a pattern that became standard, and fully developed in gnosticism. Consequently there is no explicit reference to the resurrection; the line goes directly from death to glorification. And yet, there are elements which make it different from average gnostic schemes: The obedience is decisive, and the death seems real. Most commentators consider "even the death of the cross" a Pauline addition to the hymn he quoted, and such an interpretation has been reinforced by the analysis of the metric structure of the hymn, since that phrase gives the third strophe one extra line. But metric structure in hymns of this kind is not that strict, and it is tempting to interpret the hymn in a somewhat Johannine key: . . . obedient unto death, but it was not any death, but the death of the cross, the lifting up above the earth (see above, p. 12, and below, p. 30) and *that* is why God also highly exalted him. With such an interpretation (which fits the Greek syntax better:

thanatou de staurou – dio kai), the turn toward glorification would be on the cross, as in the Johannine interpretation.

Recent studies of relevant Greek idioms now can give us a clear and meaningful translation of v. 6: ". . . though he had divine form [*morphē*; not "nature"], he did not consider the likeness to God as something to use for his own advantage . . ." (R. W. Hoover, *Harvard Theological Review* 64, 1971, pp. 95-120).

The RSV may be overly concrete when it refers to him "being born in the likeness of men." The Greek can mean both "being born" and "becoming." The NEB retains the alternatives: "Bearing the human likeness, revealed in human shape, he humbled himself . . ." And the word "humbled" is the key word of the hymn for Paul, since it is his admonition toward humility (v. 3) that leads him to the quoting of the hymn.

The hymn brings in the global note of Isa. 45:23 as the setting for the confession "Lord Jesus Christ." It is interesting to note that Paul himself uses this same quotation quite differently in Rom. 14:11. There it is the reminder of the judgment of all.

Phil. 2:5-11—Homiletical Notes. The preacher has two distinct alternatives:

1) We can meditate on the hymn, i.e., on the gracious mystery of the descent and ascent of our savior Jesus Christ. We can learn to enter into its peculiar language, retaining the mode and mood of praise and marvel and thanksgiving. And if we were in a charismatic–or at least in a less up-tight–setting, there could be many cries of "Hallelujah" and "Praise the Lord" coming from the congregation. For a hymn is a hymn and not a "text for exposition." Such a homily would be in the style: Imagine what a wonderful savior we have! And we could exemplify the verses of the hymn from the gospel stories. For example, he did not use his divine power for his own advantage: when he was hungry in the wilderness, he did not turn stones into bread, but later on, when the people were hungry, he fed them lavishly. He did not call for an army of angels to protect him, although he could have. He made himself dependent on the food and boats and rooms of others. In all these things and whatever else we can think of, he did not boast about his divinity. The divine savior honored us by wearing our clothes, lest we be blinded and discouraged by sheer transcendence.

But the *kenosis*, the impoverishment of the divine savior, did not deduct from his glory. He used his unlimited omnipotence to become limited to the human condition—even by death. He did not even rise by his own power. God had to lift him up from the dust of earth. And God liked his choice of humility and obedience so much that he superglorified him (the odd Greek word *hyperhypsōsen*, v. 8), and made him the Lord of the world and of all mankind.

2) Or there is the alternative: we could take our key from v. 5, and from Paul's specific use of this hymn for the purpose of ethical admonition. Then the hymn becomes a text for an *imitatio Christi.* How far does such an imitation go? Is Paul saying: If Christ who was divine humbled himself, how much more should you do so, being mere humans? Or is he rather saying that Christians, participating in the Spirit (v. 1), share in Christ's glory, but it is the glory of Jesus Christ who humbled himself? I think the latter is the case. Paul had found that Christians often use their faith for selfish satisfaction, what he calls *kenodoxia*, "empty conceit" (v. 3).

Perhaps we could add that true humility presupposes that we have something to be humble about. Christ certainly had. And Christians, with the Spirit and all, certainly have much to glory in. That is why true humility is possible for them, as it is also necessary for our life together.

Monday in Holy Week

Lutheran	*Roman Catholic*	*Episcopal*	*Pres./UCC/Chr.*	*Methodist/COCU*
Isa. 42:1-9	Isa. 42:1-7	Isa. 42:1-7	Isa. 50:4-10	Isa. 42:1-9
Heb. 9:11-15		Heb. 11:39-12:3	Heb. 9:11-15	Heb. 9:11-15
John 12:1-11	John 12:1-11	John 12:1-11, or Mark 14:3-9	Luke 19:41-48	John 12:1-11

Gospel: John 12:1-11—Exegesis. The anointing of the Lord belonged to the preparation for his burial. It took place in Bethany on the Mount of Olives, two miles east of Jerusalem. In Mark and Matthew it is part of the passion narrative proper (Mark 14:3-9; Matt. 26:6-13). Luke placed the parallel story in another setting (7:36-50), and there it has a different function, without any reference to the burial of Jesus, and without reflection on the woman's extravagance and its relation to the poor—this latter note was perhaps even offensive to Luke, the great champion of the poor and of almsgiving.

The Johannine text retains all the basic motifs from Mark (and Matthew), except one: There is no reference to the woman's perpetual place in the gospel as it is preached in the whole world (Mark 14:9; Matt. 26:13). But in John the story has been drawn into the Lazarus cycle, which, to John, is the link between the climax of Jesus' signs and his passion. Actually the raising of Lazarus, which pre-figures Jesus' power over death, becomes a contributing factor to his execution (John 12:9-10, 17). The reference in the tradition to Bethany (John 11:1, 18; 12:1) as the place for the anointing may also have contributed to the conflation of traditions, and John seems to be familiar with the tradition of Martha as the one doing the household chores, and of Mary as attending more religiously to the Lord, a tradition spelled out as a full story in Luke 10:38 ff. (John 12:2: "and Martha was serving").

The later traditions by which Mary (no name in the synoptics) became identified with Mary Magdalene (Luke 8:1, and the later addition to Mark, 16:9), and thus became also the repentant sinner on the basis of Luke 7:36-50, is impossible in the Gospels. To John, Mary Magdalene has her distinct role as a prime witness of the resurrection (John 20:18), and in Luke 7:37 the woman is a harlot, not one possessed by seven demons, as was his Mary Magdalene (8:2). But just as we can see in the Gospels how a web of motifs becomes conflated and suggestive, so it is not surprising that the tradition grew, hungry for more specificity, color, and identifications.

The Johannine account has its own "sinner," but following Mark and Matthew it is not the woman (only in Luke is she a sinner), but Judas (vv. 4-6). In John he is the one who makes the suggestion about selling the perfume and giving the money to the poor. John thereby lessens the dialectic of the Marcan story by making this most humane and "Christian" comment into a dishonest ploy, as he refers to Judas as the treasurer and a habitual embezzler (v. 6; cf. 13:29; the image of "Judas with the money bag" comes from John, conflated with the tradition about the 30 pieces of silver, Matt. 27:3-10).

The encounter is more straight-forward—and hence more original—in Mark and Matthew, where the motives are good, compassionate, and reasonable when the disciples make that same suggestion. In the story so told Jesus' answer has a clear point: This is a very special moment, and this woman's exuberant devotion fits right into God's drama at this point. His response to her impulse of extreme generosity is beautiful. Do not use rational arguments against it. In the Marcan account there is even an echo from the story about the widow's mite: "What she had, she used" (Mark 14:8; cf. 12:44).

This same message remains in John, and it is interesting to note how basically his account of Mary's exuberance functions as a true parallel to Luke's story about Martha and Mary (10:38-42). Mary's irresponsible attitude of devotion without practical responsibility is glorified, over against Martha's busy-ness and/or the disciples' concern for the poor.

John 12:1-11—Homiletical Notes. The main theme for the meditation and/or sermon is clear: There is a place and a time for what wise people must consider excessive and reckless exuberance and "waste." The authentic act of devotion must be guarded against the rational planners —lest we lose our humanity. The woman (Mary) followed her feelings without calculation. And it so happened that her act fitted precisely into the drama of salvation: It became part of Christ's preparation for death. As Lazarus' return to life prefigured that of Jesus, so his sister Mary's act prefigured his burial. She did not intend it that way, she just acted out her devotion without forethought or planning, but such acts are used by God.

What about the poor? Does not this story encourage more gold in the cathedrals and less energy in social action? Of course it could, and it has. For humans will always try to use God's word to their advantage. Therefore, we can well imagine Jesus and his disciples in the reverse position, with the disciples saying: We must first pay homage to you, Lord, and then we shall give to the poor what is left over—and Jesus answering: What you have done for them you have done for me, and you had better start with them. Actually there is such a story in the Gospels: It is the story of the Good Samaritan with its religionists eager to get to the temple uncontaminated. Luke was perhaps conscious of the interplay of these two tendencies as he placed "The Good Samaritan" and "Martha and Mary" together (10:29-42).

But now, in Holy Week, the emphasis is on the unique moment and on the exuberant generosity and devotion.

In the Church of Sweden this text cannot be read in Holy Week without one's hearing in the background a passion hymn by Nathan Soederblom. It reads (in prose translation):

> See how the flask is broken and the ointment spent;
> Its scent fills the world's house of mourning.
> Your soul, surrounded by heavenly fragrance,
> Is lifted out of dust and earth.
>
> Let the flask be broken, let its nardus flow,
> Be not greedy, prepare your soul for the feast.
> Let love lavish the very best it has
> On your soul's most glorious guest.

First Lesson: Isa. 42:1-9—Exegesis. This is the first of the Songs of the Servant (vv. 1-4) and the response thereto (vv. 5-9); cf. comments above to Isa. 50:4-9 (p. 19). The NT reader is very familiar with this text. Matthew brings it into his Gospel to underline by prophecy Jesus' order to avoid publicity for his miracles (Matt. 12:18-21).

This Servant Song has no note of suffering; it rather stresses the gentle and compassionate style of this Servant in contrast to the shrill proclamations and power displays of the world. The main theme of the Song and the echoing response, however, is the mission of the Servant as the one through whom Yahweh–the creator of the whole world, the animator of all nature–goes far beyond Israel, and through whom his law and judgment are brought to the gentiles, to the "coastlands" (KJV: isles, i.e., the coastal region of Syria and Phoenicia, for the Israelites a remote area at the limits of the earth). This outreach is not thought of as a conquering imperialism–the Servant does not practice violence and coercion, but brings the word with quiet determination, trusting in God who chose him and sent him. Thus he is not to sit in judgment over them, rather he brings Torah, i.e., guidance and instruction.

The covenant with Israel is seen as a call to her to be a beacon, a light for the nations, the gentiles; and the Servant is the agent through whom this light is now quickly but irresistibly to be brought to them. When Jesus used this word in Matt. 5:14, it was presumably addressed to Israel: "You are the light of the world . . .", but transferred by Matthew to the disciples.

Isa. 42:1-9—Homiletical Notes. In Holy Week this Servant Song takes on special meaning. As the Second Lesson (from Hebrews, see below) lifts the events of the passion up into the heavenly sphere and interprets Jesus' death as the sacrifice that transcends all sacrifices, so Isa. 42 brings in the global perspective: the gospel is to be brought to the uttermost parts of the world (Acts 1:8), the invitation to discipleship goes out to all nations and cultures (Matt. 28:19). This motif leads over strongly to Tuesday's Gospel (John 12:20-36; see below).

In Holy Week it may be both easier and more appropriate to remember that this global outreach through the Servant is not triumphalistic. Perhaps Israel's understanding of her mission as a light for the gentiles has much to teach us. Their witness to the One God and to the moral order is a witness, not a drive toward conversion in the human sense. Such matters are in the hands of God. Isaiah does not say that the gentiles will become Jews (or Christians). He is not interested in statistics or ecclesiastical expansion. He has only one aim: that the Law, the Torah, reach the coastlands and that the voice of justice and truth be heard.

Second Lesson: Hebrews 9:11-15—Exegesis. In the Epistle to the Hebrews the meaning of Jesus Christ is presented under the image of priesthood and sacrifice. The continuity and the decisive newness are elaborated in a manner and in thought patterns that we know well from the Alexandrian Jewish philosopher Philo (born ca. 25 B.C.) and which have their closest NT parallels in Stephen's speech (Acts 7) with its negative reading of the temple "made with hands" (v. 48).

The Christ of Hebrews is the Son, hence higher than the angels (1:5–2:18), he is the faithful and compassionate High Priest (3:1–5:10) whose priesthood is eternal (5:11–7:28), after the order of Melchizedek ("without father or mother or genealogy, and has neither beginning of days nor end of life, but resembling the Son of God he continues a priest forever," 7:3), and whose sacrifice is eternal and hence not in need of repetition, 9:12 (8:1–9:28).

In the Greek text of Heb. 9:11-14 there are only two main verbs; everything else is expressed by participles or in other dependent ways: "He *entered* the sanctuary once for all" (v. 12); "and the blood of Christ will *cleanse* our [so the better manuscripts; KJV, RSV: "your"] conscience from dead deeds" (v. 14). Thereby the image is clear. It requires as background reading Lev. 16 concerning the great annual Day of Atonement (Yom Kippur), and also the laws about the red heifer (Num. 19, see esp. v. 17 for the use of ashes for cleansing, Heb. 9:13, and also the reference to "outside the camp," Num. 19:3, cf. Heb. 13:13).

The reading "high priest of good things to come" (9:11, KJV) is based on inferior manuscripts; the best texts refer to "the good things that have come" (so RSV; cf. NEB). The better tabernacle (v. 11) does not refer to the Body of Christ as the heavenly temple, but to the heavenly regions through which Christ entered into heaven itself (9:24; cf. 4:14, in the Second Lesson for Good Friday, see below).

What the ritual of the Atonement accomplished in a manner needing constant repetition is now accomplished in a cosmic and eternal, i.e., lasting manner. The sacrificial cult is transcended and thereby made obsolete as the heavenly high priest has offered himself. Our consciences are now cleansed from acts tainted by the order of earth and death (cf. 9:9), true service and worship are possible (cf. Rom. 12:1, and Heb. 13:18; cf. also John 4:23), and the new covenant has been ratified (vv. 15 ff.; cf. Jer. 31:31-34).

Hebrews 9:11-15—Homiletical Notes. When Hebrews presents the work of Christ under the image of sacrifice and sacrificial priesthood, we should note what I would call both sides of such a message.

One side is relatively easy for us to grasp and accept: By the drama of Calvary all sacrifices have been made obsolete. We need not bring sacrifices to God in order to placate him. The sacrificial cult has ceased. This line of reasoning is often coupled with feelings of spiritual and cultural superiority over against so-called primitive ideas and practices of sacrifices, and the need of placating the gods by such acts. Judaism has had her own development of overcoming the practice of sacrifices, governed by the prophetic critique of sacrificial cult (cf. Ps. 50:12, see below). Christians speak of thanksgiving as the proper and enlightened sacrifice to God. And all this is good and sound and spiritually valid.

But the other side of the coin is not to be forgotten: Christ's death is a sacrifice. It would be nice if that were not so. It would be nice if the world were such, if reality were such, that no sacrifices were needed. When Hebrews sees the death of Christ as a sacrifice, it reminds us of the fact that Christian faith cannot be grasped in its depth without the ancient and "primitive" act of sacrifice to God for the people.

It is usually true in the life and thought of religions—and Christianity is no exception—that the deepest experiences and insights are to be found in the most "primitive," i.e., fundamental and lasting forms and myths and practices. Sacrifice surely is one of those.

Did God need to be satisfied by a sacrifice of his Son? No, God needs nothing: "If I were hungry, I would not tell you; for the world and all that is in it is mine. Do I eat the flesh of bulls . . ." (Ps. 50:12). Before the cross we should not ask: Did it have to be this way? In his omnipotence God could fashion his salvation in billions of ways. But when we meditate on what actually happened, then we see the sacrifice on Calvary. And we ask: What are you telling us, Lord? Hebrews gives us one answer. There is the sacrifice of sacrifices. It speaks about our sins atoned for and our deliverance into a new covenant. On Good Friday the fourth Servant song (Isa. 53) will give its answer as Christians read about how "like a lamb he was led to the slaughter, and like a sheep, dumb before its shearers, he opened not his mouth," and how "he was wounded for our transgressions."

Tuesday in Holy Week

Lutheran	*Roman Catholic*	*Episcopal*	*Pres./UCC/Chr.*	*Methodist/COCU*
Isa. 49:1-6	Isa. 49:1-6	Isa. 49:1-9*a*	Isa. 42:1-9	Isa. 49:1-9a
1 Cor. 1:18-25		1 Cor. 1:18-31	1 Tim. 6:11-16	1 Cor. 1:18-31
John 12:20-36	John 13:21-33, 36-38	John 12:37-38, 42-50	John 12:37-50	John 12:37-50

Gospel: John 12:20-36—Exegesis. In John the momentum of the following of Jesus is strong after his seventh and final sign, the raising of Lazarus (chap. 11). Crowds come out of Jerusalem to meet him (12:13), and there is the witness of the crowd that has seen Lazarus raised (v. 18). Even some of the authorities believe in him (v. 42), and the Pharisees are in despair and find themselves unable to do anything: "Look, the world [*ho kosmos*] has taken off after him" (v. 19).

This global success is further exemplified by the coming of "some Greeks." They seem to be non-Jews, but godfearers (cf. Acts 16:14). They approach Jesus through the two disciples with Greek names and from a town on the border of Gentile territory (Bethsaida, east of the Jordan). John does not describe a meeting between Jesus and these Greeks; he seems to retain the image of Jesus' earthly ministry as confined to the Jews; rather his answer looks toward the time when he as the glorified Son will transcend such limits. That hour is the hour of his being lifted up on the cross–his glorification: "And I, when [the KJV translates the Greek literally "if," but the syntax indicates no uncertainty] I am lifted up, shall draw all to me" (v. 32; cf. John 10:16).

This hour of glorification appears to the world as a death, and John has brought together at this point traditional elements that the synoptic Gospels have preserved otherwise. In John, the word about losing and gaining one's life (related to the words about how to follow Jesus and his cross in Mark 8:35 par.) refers primarily to Jesus' own death: "As the grain falls in the ground . . .", vv. 24 f.; cf. 1 Cor. 15:35 ff. And there is a rare element of inner turmoil in Jesus, but none of the agony in Gethsemane. Jesus knows the purpose of this hour to be his "glorification," and the heavenly voice (like in the synoptics at the baptism and transfiguration of Jesus; cf. the strengthening angel in Gethsemane, Luke 22:43) is not needed by Jesus, but is for the benefit of the disciples (v. 30).

Vv. 31-36 now bring in a mighty Johannine theme, already presented in the speech to Nicodemus (chap. 3). The famous words "God so loved the world that he gave his only begotten Son . . ." (3:16) are John's interpretation of the crucifixion of Jesus according to the prophetic image of the serpent in the wilderness: "As Moses lifted up the serpent . . ." (3:14). In both cases the effect is "life" (Num. 21:8 f.; John 3:15, 16). And in chap. 3 that text continues with the words about "judgment" and "light."

Thus what is given in John 3 in terms of ideas, now is beginning to happen. In the perspective of Jesus' ministry these are the last moments for choosing the light, but the leaders who leaned toward Jesus (v. 42) did show that they loved darkness rather than light (3:19). The darkness overwhelmed them (v. 35, the same expression as in John 1:5, and one of the reasons why most translations do not favor the KJV's translation of that verse: "and the darkness comprehended it not").

At this point the public ministry of Jesus ends ("he hid himself," v. 36); it ends on the borderline to his global glory, of which he speaks when he hears that the Greeks are beginning to come.

John 12:20-36—Homiletical Notes. The text is rich in words and motifs for meditation. I would perhaps try to communicate the theme that holds the whole text together: Death is the only way to new life. In our text—very differently from 1 Cor. 15—this principle of the grain that must die refers to Jesus and his mission, and consequently also to the church and her mission and work. What does it mean for the church, for Christianity, to die? It seems to be the only way to life. Should we perhaps think about how Christianity gets entangled in culture and prestige and status? The more glorious its "wheat" looks to people, the more limited and polluted by Western imperialism, etc., becomes the gospel. The church must die or her life in all its glory cannot live on, and she has not the right word for "the Greeks," i.e., for those of other cultural habits of thought and experience. But we are afraid of syncretism and the loss of Christian orthodoxy and identity. Yes, but the living continuity is according to the law of the grain that dies, not by our letting the grain shine in our hand.

Or we could fasten on v. 32—which says the same thing under the image of the Serpent—and we could bring in John 3:16 and enliven that famous verse by painting the image of Moses who raised up the Serpent as a means toward life. We would remember that the gift was not that the snakes disappeared, but that those who were bitten looked to the stake with the body and stayed alive. For Lutherans it is natural to remember that salvation is not the bliss of sinlessness. The snakes keep biting, but there is a means by which their venom is not deadly.

But John would rather stress how the cross and death of Christ are the means by which Jesus transcends the limitations of all cultural, national, and religious boundaries: "I have other sheep, that are not of this fold; I must bring them also" (John 10:16). This Jesus, lifted up, is not the founder of a religion, the originator of a tradition. He is unlimited, like God.

First Lesson: Isa. 49:1-6—Exegesis. Now the second of the Songs of the Servant of Yahweh, and this time without the "response" (vv. 7-13). Again, as in the first song (see Monday, above), the theme is the Servant as the agent through whom Yahweh reaches out beyond the confines of the tribes of Israel. The striking features are: (1) the sense of call, expressed partly in the language of Jeremiah (1:5, also used by Paul about his call to apostleship, Gal. 1:15), and partly with unique imagery of trust (v. 2); and (2) the strange reference to Israel in v. 3, considered by many interpreters as a later gloss. Even with poetic oscillation it is an awkward reference, since v. 5 makes Israel an object of the Servant's work. But in the "response" the Servant clearly is Israel; cf. below, on the lesson for Good Friday.

The greatness of the Servant is expressed by the extension of his mission to the whole world, and his frustration but not despair concerning the results of his work is overcome by this far greater assignment. The theme clearly enunciated in the first song is here celebrated from the personal perspective of the Servant, reflecting on his call, his trust, his frustrations, and the greatness of his mission.

Isa. 49:1-6—Homiletical Notes. This text from Isaiah may serve well to illustrate that "outreach" of which the Gospel for this day speaks. In using the text in such a fashion we should be aware of how, again, the Servant's trust in the Lord goes counter to what he sees with his eyes and feels in his bones, i.e., perhaps counter to what the statistics and Gallup polls and balance sheets say: "I have labored in vain, I have spent my strength for nothing and vanity" (v. 4).

All these texts from Isaiah speak against the only secularization that is truly bad: The secularization of the church. By that I mean the tendency–it is often more than a tendency, I am afraid–of Christians to count growth and outreach and results in quantitative terms. Church statistics have their function. If they are honest, they help pastors and congregations to keep honest about their work, but they can never be used as a measurement for the secret growth of the kingdom.

The Servant, the church, the Christian base their hope and ground their service in the call of God and await God's result beyond human failure and success. As Jesus said to the justifiably achievement-happy disciples: "Rejoice not in the fact that the (evil) spirits are subject to you; but rejoice that your names are written in heaven" (Luke 10:20; cf. John 15:15). Such words and attitudes may appear self-centered, but not when they function as a warning against secular hunting for results. The call and the promise are part of that warning, and they are words of encouragement for the downcast. But when they are worn by the proud and successful as medals and badges they turn to ashes.

We should also meditate in awe and gratitude on how this and the other Servant songs remain truly meaningful for Israel, for the Jews, as they reflect on their high servanthood among the nations, often under the sign of bondage (v. 7), "deeply despised, abhorred by the gentiles," among whom so-called Christians have been found more often than not.

Second Lesson: 1 Cor. 1:18-25—Exegesis. Here we get a glimpse into Paul's way of speaking about the cross. Actually, Paul does so less often than is our impression from memory and expectation. For example, the word does not occur in Romans (except "co-crucified," as an interpretation of baptism, 6:6). When he uses the word, it is always in a critique of certain types of Christian piety which he considers dangerous. Luther understood this well when he distinguished between a *theologia crucis* and *theologia gloriae* (theologies of the cross and of glory).

In his Corinthian correspondence Paul tries hard to combat the *theologia gloriae* of some Christian teachers who seem to have fascinated people in that church. They presented the gospel as Wisdom—not the common-sense wisdom of Proverbs, but Wisdom as deep and revealed speculation and insight, attractive to the Hellenistic world. Paul claims that Christ himself is that Wisdom, not speculations about him (chap. 2). These Christian teachers presented themselves as charismatic wonderworkers, performing signs and encouraging ecstatic manifestations to which Paul gives his response in 1 Cor. 12-14, placing the concern for the weak and the building up of the community ("love") above both faith and knowledge.

According to Paul, all such tendencies are dangerous. They grow out of a faith that has not taken the cross seriously. They undermine the power and message of the cross (1 Cor. 1:17). Or rather, he finds the image of the crucifixion to be the antidote to such tendencies. The salvation Christ brought came into the world not with celestial signs satisfying Jewish expectations or according to the specifications of the wise and the learned. The last in wisdom and power became the first to see and believe (vv. 26-31). Christ's coming was ironic, the foolishness of a Messiah crucified in weakness (2 Cor. 13:4) is the power of God, available to those who have eyes to see. In the gospel of the cross, irony becomes the key to salvation. That is also why these verses are written in the literary style called irony.

Here is the polemic expression of that insight of Paul's which most of all permeates his writings: over against heroic models of successful spirituality he stresses that the Christian, even the true apostle, Paul himself, is part of the groaning creation, saved only in hope (Rom. 8:18-26), and that our weakness alone allows the power of God to shine forth (2 Cor. 12:10; cf. 4:7).

1 Cor. 1:18-25—Homiletical Notes. This passage should not be the occasion for thundering against science and learning in the academic world, nor for general and popular reflections on "faith and knowledge." Both the "signs" and the "wisdom" that Paul has in mind are the expression of deeply religious attitudes of faith. The *skandalon* (offense) of the cross (Gal. 5:11) is not difficult for the *world* to understand. They have no difficulty in seeing how small and pitiful Jesus and his followers are. (We must remember that Paul does not refer to the resurrection, which may well be such a stumbling block to "the world.") It is for the triumphalist and deeply religious spiritualists, the heavy believers that the cross, the defeat, the disgrace, the weakness of Jesus Christ is such a *skandalon*.

Thus our sermon and meditation should have that same focus and address. It should be against our tendencies toward overstating our power and bliss and "saved-ness." It should be against claiming more for our faith than is true. It should be centered around the question: Are we willing to accept the irony of God's ways, i.e., to expect no victory for ourselves or for our Christian usefulness to the world, to become like the Servant (Isa. 42), and to wait in our weakness for God's Easter which may not come to us in five days? The question must be: Are our faith, our piety, our conscious and unconscious view of ourselves and our problems shaped by the cross to the extent that we are willing to wait for God without signs, and self-serving rationalization, and self-glorifying pious rhetoric? The question is: Are we willing to keep silent like the Lord before his accusers, "trusting in him who judges justly" (1 Peter 2:23)?

Wednesday in Holy Week

Lutheran	*Roman Catholic*	*Episcopal*	*Pres./UCC/Chr.*	*Methodist/COCU*
Isa. 50:4–9*a*	Isa. 50:4–9*a*	Isa. 50:4–9*a*	Isa. 52:13–53:12	Isa. 50:4–9
Rom. 5:6–11		Heb. 9:11–15, 24–28	Rom. 5:6–11	Rom. 5:6–11
Matt. 26:14–25	Matt. 26:14–25	Matt. 26:1–5, 14–25	Luke 22:1–16	Matt. 26:14–25

Gospel: Matt. 26:14-25—Exegesis. We have already had reason to offer exegetical observations to these three short sections of Matthew as we tried to bring out what is peculiar to Matthew (see above, pp. 15-16).

The Judas figure is made more distinct, and also more personal, by Matthew. His approach to the high priests is given in direct speech (v. 15), and he himself asks whether he is the traitor (v. 25). The reference to the thirty silver coins (v. 15) prepares for the actions and the rabbinic exegesis of the high priests later on (27:3-10).

Was Judas a participant in the meal when Jesus said that the wine was his blood poured out for many to the forgiveness of sins (the last five words only in Matt., 26:28)? It seems that the evangelists were not concerned about that question, although it has played a very significant role in the history of eucharistic theology and the theology of sin and grace. In John, Judas departs into the darkness of night after Jesus has said: "What you are doing, do quickly" (13:27), but John has no institution of a eucharist. Luke places the prediction of the betrayal after the meal (22:21-23), and thus Judas had been there all the time. In Mark and Matthew there is no indication that Judas had left earlier.

In Matthew alone the preparation for the passover meal has the majestic ring of Jesus' "self-invitation": The Teacher says "My time is close at hand. It is in your house that I celebrate Passover with my disciples" (v. 18). The reference to the time (*kairos*) heightens the drama.

Matt. 26:14-25—Homiletical Notes. The text gives us a stark image of how Jesus, in full command, prepares for the Passover to which he would give a very special meaning, tying it together with his death and the messianic banquet in the kingdom to come. And we see Jesus' majestic way of showing how he is aware of the betrayal to come through the acts of Judas.

Here is an image of how Jesus handles radical evil. Matthew does not describe how Jesus felt–the feelings are those of the disciples (v. 22). The style is terse. Jesus does not warn or judge or attempt to win Judas back. It is too late. He just states what will happen and answers Judas in a way which only the two of them understand.

Thus there is evil in this world beyond mending and bending. It has to be. It does not come from God. But somehow it can be fitted into God's plan of salvation. The mystery of evil remains a mystery. The omnipotence of God is not a babysitting omnipotence. Nor are we taught that God "allows" evil; that is a rationalization and one which becomes plain unbearable–think for example about the killing of millions of Jews in the death camps.

Just as in the story of the fall (Gen. 3), so also here: Evil is there, and we are not told where it came from. The Christian way is to recognize it–and to trust that God is strong and wise enough to press good wine even out of the grapes of wrath and deceit.

Perhaps we could say that Jesus says to Judas what Joseph had said to his brothers: "As for you, you thought evil against me, but God thought/will think it into good, to bring it about that many people be given life. . ." (Gen. 50:20).

Our sermon could well dwell on this mystery of evil, refraining from our rationalizations, as we learn how Jesus faced radical evil, even among those closest to him.

First Lesson: Isa. 50:4-9a (See exegesis and homiletical notes for Passion Sunday, above, pp. 19-21.)

Second Lesson: Rom. 5:6-11—Exegesis. This section in Paul's letter to the Romans is a prime example of what is called *anakolouthon*, i.e., a style with interrupted flow and awkward syntax. The thoughts and images come over Paul as he dictates. The Greek text gives a strong impression of an abundance of thought that he cannot easily structure—all the translators have smoothed over this. Do look up the Greek to get the feel of the passage.

This "disorder" can be a sign of strong emotion. It can also be due to

Paul's eagerness to bring in many of his favorite topics and themes. Just as in Rom. 8 so also here, Paul cannot speak about the Christian status of bliss, peace, and access to God and to glory (cf. Rom. 5:1-2), without stressing that such glorying is only "in hope," and in the midst of tribulations (*thlipseis*, v. 3; cf. 8:18), and that the Spirit is the sign of this sustaining power of hope (v. 5; cf. 8:24-27 about glossolalia).

The love of God is realistic and trustworthy since it comes to us not in our strength, as an approval or reward for our being strong, pious, and devoted. The structure of God's salvation is rather to have let Christ die for sinners, enemies, and the weak.

We should also note that here—as always in Paul—salvation is in the future (always future tense). Justification and reconciliation have been achieved; they are wrought by the death and blood of Christ. Salvation, the consummation of the process, is yet to come. In a very specific sense Paul lives in Holy Week, and for him it is important that our salvation, our "risen life," is of the future. Later Christian theology—following Paul's opponents—did away with this distinction, which was so important to him.

We can read our passage as an exulting in what God has wrought in Christ—and we are right in doing so. But the very structure of the passage is rather aimed at saying: Faith is trouble—with a hope for future salvation. It is a good and sure hope since so much has been done already and since we have learned about Christ that he caters to sinners, weaklings, and even enemies by reconciliation and justification. Thus we can look with confidence to the outcome—in spite of our troubles. We glory in being already (v. 11) reconciled with God. But the full life and implementation are yet to come.

We should note that the word "reconciliation" (*katallagē/katallassō*) is never used in Paul—or any other NT writer—for reconciliation between persons (except once, in the case of an estranged couple, 1 Cor. 7:11). It expresses the reconciliation with God. Why is that so? Perhaps Paul felt it to be such an enormous matter that he did not find it natural to use it for the overcoming of human enmity. When that is the issue he speaks about love.

Rom. 5:6-11—Homiletical Notes. A possible theme is: In his love God could not wait any longer. That is why Christ died for sinners, the weak, and enemies. That is why the Spirit comes to those who are not properly worthy. The love of God is his lack of patience: Final salvation must wait, of course; that belongs to the day of consummation; but I shall give them all I can, justification, reconciliation, the Spirit as the foretaste of the bliss of heaven.

This "lack of patience" on God's part, this graciousness, has its risks. Paul knew it, and we should know it. The rejoicing in God can lead to boasting. The Greek word (*kauchaomai*) that RSV translates by "rejoicing" is the same that Paul often uses in the sense of boasting (e.g., 1 Cor. 1:29). To Paul such boasting is a grave sin. So we must figure out how our faith can be rejoicing without becoming boasting. In Holy Week that line is perhaps easier to draw. The participants in the drama all fall short, by overt actions or miserable inaction, and that goes for the disciples also. They all are weak sinners, enemies or playing into the hands of the enemies. The passion story is the stark and classical moment, "the right time" for Christ to die for the ungodly.

Maundy Thursday

Lutheran	*Roman Catholic*	*Episcopal*	*Pres./UCC/Chr.*	*Methodist/COCU*
Exod. 12:1–14	Exod. 12:1–8, 11–14	Exod. 12:1–14*a*	Exod. 12:1–8, 11–14	Exod. 12:1–14
1 Cor. 11:23–26	1 Cor. 11:23–26	1 Cor. 11:23–26	1 Cor. 11:23–32	1 Cor. 11:23–26
John 13:1–17	John 13:1–15	John 13:1–15, or Luke 22:14–30	John 13:1–15	John 13:1–15

With the Gospel text from John 13:1-17, this year has a real "Maundy" Thursday, the Thursday of the *mandatum (novum)*, the new commandment of mutual love (13:34), exemplified by the footwashing which Jesus commanded his disciples to practice (13:14 f.). In various forms such an observance has been part of the church's celebration of Holy Week through the ages, and its symbolism was striking enough to lead to the popular naming of this day. It still is a beautiful thing when carried out in a natural manner—as among people with dungarees and sandals. Bourgeois habits of dress do not fit too well—but I guess Jesus and his disciples did not dress up in coat and tie when they went to the meal.

The three texts of Maundy Thursday broaden the understanding of the eucharist and its relation to the Jewish Passover. The First (OT) Lesson gives us the "words of institution" for the Passover, the epistle Second Lesson gives us the Pauline "words of institution" for what Paul calls the Lord's Meal (*deipnon kyriakon*, a *deipnon* is the main meal of the day, or a formal meal, a banquet), and the Gospel presents "words of institution" for a ritual of footwashing, given at a meal which is not a Passover meal and which has no reference to an institution of a eucharist. In order to further broaden the perspective and add to the richness of motifs that belong to the Meal of the church, we also remember the instructions from the Didache, chap. 9 (The Teaching of the Apostles, ca. A.D. 100-150): "Concerning the Eucharist [thanksgiving] celebrate it [give thanks] in this manner: First concerning the cup: We give you thanks, our Father, for the holy vine of David your child [or: servant], for the vine that you made known to us through Jesus your child [or: servant]. Glory to you for ages! And concerning the broken bread: We give you thanks, our Father, for the life and knowledge that you made known to us through Jesus your child [or: servant]. Glory to you for ages!—As this broken bread was scattered upon the mountains and became one when assembled, so let your church be assembled from the ends of the earth into your kingdom, for the glory and the power are yours through Jesus Christ for ages" (see also the Didache's prayer after the eucharist, chap. 10).

With this material before us we shall find how the Meal, the central cultic act of the church (cf. Acts 2:42 and 46), became a magnet for many motifs and how the meal "on the night when he was handed over" (1 Cor. 11:23), was never the "last supper," but an event that gave special meaning to the meal fellowship that had been part of their life as disciples, was transcended in the feeding of the multitudes, was drawn into the sphere of the Passover, was the meal of longing for Christ's coming in glory ("until he come"), and retained and developed many other connotations in the experience of the church.

Gospel: John 13:1-17—Exegesis. Actually the evening meal here described is not a Passover meal. In John's chronology Good Friday falls on the day when the Passover meal was eaten in the evening, and the meal at which Jesus demonstrated his abiding love to the disciples (13:1) is on the preceding evening (cf. 13:29; 18:28; 19:14, 31, 42). It is possible that this Johannine chronology has a conscious symbolism of presenting the death of Jesus as the slaughtered "Lamb of God that takes away the sins of the world" (John 1:29, 36; 19:14, 36; the passover lambs were slaughtered at noon), even if the passover lambs were not an offering for sins. Various attempts at explaining this Johannine chronology by a solar calendar, possibly used by Jewish sects, and now found at Qumran, versus the lunar calendar of Jerusalem, are not convincing in the light of John's obvious interest in symbolism. John pictures Jesus consistently as the true and full manifestation of that which the Jewish feasts celebrated (e.g., 7:2, 37 ff.; and 10:22 ff.).

John's eucharistic teaching is not part of his passion narrative, but is found within the extended discourse(s) after the feeding of the multitudes (chap. 6). There is a reference to the time of Passover (6:3), and this may not be a later addition, since John often gives the Jewish festivals as the setting for Jesus' acts and words (2:12; 2:23; 4:45; 5:1; 11:55, and the passages referred to above). But the following seventy-one verses have no reference to the Passover proper. The operative image from the OT is rather the manna in the wilderness (from v. 31 on).

The section most directly related to the eucharist is in vv. 51-59. Jesus is the true manna from heaven which gives eternal life; he is the living bread that has descended from heaven. He teaches about the necessity of eating his flesh. He intensifies the sacramental language by speaking about "flesh"—not "body" as in the synoptics and in Paul—and by using the word *trōgō* (munch, eat audibly [German: *fressen*], 6:54 ff.; he even brings that word into the quotation from Ps. 41:10, this against the LXX *ho estiōn*, "he who ate", 13:18). Of course, this whole discourse also has a metaphorical meaning, and to eat the flesh from heaven is to accept and believe (6:28 f.), but at the same time there is the stark and anti-spiritualistic stress on the necessity of sacramental participation.

But John's eucharist is not tied to the night when Jesus was handed over. It was not instituted in the setting of the Passover meal. The last meal Jesus and the disciples had together got its character from the great example of Jesus' humble and loving service in the washing of the disciples' feet. His farewell gift was the New Commandment (13:34), and the loving teaching and prayer of departure (chaps. 14-17).

Again John stresses how Jesus knows all that is to happen and is aware of his fate and glorification (13:1, 3, 11, 18). The scene reminds us of the synoptic teaching of Jesus against concern for status (Luke 22:24-28; Matt. 23:12; cf. Matt. 10:24 par., and Luke 12:37), but in John this teaching is expressed in an actual act by Jesus, to be repeated by the disciples.

The exchange between Simon Peter and Jesus (vv. 6-11) is not easy to understand, and any interpretation must be tentative. John has such a delightful way of operating on many levels. The richness of his writing lies partly in the undertones and the overtones. Peter's first objection is clearly meant to signal the reversal of roles between master and disciples, i.e., the theme in vv. 13-17; his lack of understanding reminds us of Mark 8:32 f. par. Perhaps the exchange brings in a distinction between what the footwashing symbolizes and baptism (the verb for "he who has bathed," *louomai*, is used for baptism in 1 Cor. 6:11; Eph. 5:26; Titus 3:5; Heb. 10:22; *niptō*, "wash" is not so used in the NT). If so, then the footwashing is a symbolic act by which Jesus transmits the gospel of mutual and serving love. To refuse it is to deny the true nature of Jesus as the loving master. For the already purified (cf. John 15:3) only the acceptance and the practice of this rule of love and service are needed, but without it they have "no part" in Jesus (v. 8).

First Lesson: Exodus 12:1-14—Exegesis. The Passover is the great feast of liberation from the slavery in Egypt. It is the beginning of the march toward Sinai and the reception of the Law, the Law that begins with the words "I am Yahweh, your God, who brought you out of the land of Egypt, out of the house of bondage . . ." (Exod. 20:2). Passover is the feast of the protection of Israel in an alien land when Yahweh "passes over" her houses in the night of judgment. It is a joyous feast, yet one eaten "in haste," in preparedness for departure. It is the Jewish festival most tied to a historical memory—one of momentous significance.

The roots go further back, into the nomadic past and the sacrifice of lambs. The sacrifice of lambs became wedded to the agricultural feast of settled people, the Seven days of the Unleavened Bread (Exod. 12:15; cf. Mark 14:1 par.).

In the time of Jesus it was the great occasion for pilgrimage to Jerusalem (cf. Luke 2:41). In the Jewish celebration of Passover there is the hopeful prayer through thousands of years in exile: "Next Passover in Jerusalem!"

When the Christian faith and story became intertwined with Passover, a powerful and often ugly chapter opened up. The worst forms of anti-semitism fastened to this feast, the most devastating pogroms were staged in Holy Week, fanned by the story of Christ's last Passover in Jerusalem.

In our reading of Exod. 12, we must therefore listen carefully to the fullness of the message of Passover in its original power and beauty. Also for a Christian—as for Jesus—this feast has its own distinct message. According to the synoptic Gospels, the last meal with Jesus was a full Passover. That is not reported in detail; it is just taken for granted. When Jesus used the occasion of that Passover for the prophetic sign of his impending death, he added a new dimension; he did not invalidate the Passover.

Thus there is much wisdom and hope for spiritual renewal and new understanding of our debt to Judaism when Christians today begin again to celebrate the Seder—the Passover meal. And if our Jewish friends can find it in their hearts to join with us and we with them in such a Passover—in spite of almost 2000 years of Christian slander and worse—then we can praise God together for his acts of liberation in times of trouble.

Second Lesson: 1 Cor. 11:17-32 (long); 1 Cor. 11:23-26 (short)—Exegesis. The shorter alternative gives the Pauline form of the words of institution, followed by the Pauline emphasis on the cross and on the "not yet" of the consummation (cf. exegesis of 1 Cor. 1:18-25, above). While the formulation is Paul's, both motifs are an integral part of all three synoptic accounts: ". . . until that day when I drink it new in the kingdom of God" (Mark 14:25, par.; cf. also Luke 22:28-30).

Paul presents his words of institution as tradition with the immediate authority of the Lord. While the synoptic Gospels give such words in the actual setting of the last evening and of a Passover meal, Paul's form is more stylized, with more perfect parallelism between bread and cup. There is no reference to the Passover, only to the night when he was handed over (Greek imperfect tense: the whole string of events leading up to that), and Paul's interpretation does not utilize any specific Passover motifs. In details he is closest to the Lukan form: This is my body *for you*—in my remembrance—this cup is the new covenant in my blood. And the cup is taken "after he had supped."

But it is the whole passage beginning in v. 17 and including also vv. 32-34 that helps us to understand what is so important to Paul in the celebration of the meal. In 10:14-22 this celebration furnished Paul with the distinction between "the cup and table of the Lord" and "the cup and table of demons"—in answer to the question about *participation* in heathen feasts.

The catchword is *koinōnia/koinōnos,* the word which gave us the term "communion" for the eucharist. KJV uses "communion" and "fellowship" here, but the Vulgate was closer when it translated *communicatio* and *participatio,* for there is no reference to fellowship (communion) between or among people. Paul never uses the term *koinōnia* in that sense. It refers to participation, sharing in holy things—or to the collection (Rom. 15:26). The same may be true for Acts 2:42, where the *koinōnia* may not refer to general fellowship but to "the communion," i.e., the breaking of bread (the Vulgate reads *et communicatione fractionis panis,* "and the participation in the breaking of bread"). All this indicates that originally the term "communion" was a reference to the participation in divine things and acts and powers. The English words "fellowship" and "communion" were used for that participation and sharing—as also in the blessing "The grace of the Lord Jesus Christ and the fellowship (KJV: communion) of the Holy Spirit be with you all" (2 Cor. 13:13). To modern readers the horizontal and social connotation of these words became overwhelming and often pushed aside the primary meaning: The sacramental participation, sharing in the Lord and his gifts.

In 1 Cor. 11, however, Paul has reasons to express in his own way the consequences for the community of this holy participation. He does so by reflecting not on the words "fellowship/communion," but on the meaning of Christ as the Body (*sōma*).

The Corinthians may not have taken very seriously the problem which Paul perceives. The picture is clear. Those who come early with their supplies to the common meal begin to eat the food they have brought before all have arrived. Perhaps the servants and slaves could not come until rather late, and they could not bring food, for that would be stealing. This is obviously the issue as can be seen from Paul's practical advice: Wait for one another, and if you are that hungry, eat a sandwich at home before you go (vv. 33 f.; cf. v. 22). But to Paul this misbehavior is not a small thing. He sees it as a deadly sin against the Body of Christ: they do not recognize the Body (v. 29; cf. 12:12, 27), i.e., the true nature of the church. They have not understood what the

Lord's Supper is about, but make it seem a selfish meal without sharing with the poor, thereby "showing contempt for the church" (vv. 21 f.).

It is this very specific situation that causes Paul to remind them of the words of institution. For the meal is a sacred feast and the very act by which they become one with the body and blood of Christ by which the new covenant is established. It is the memorial sacrifice of the Lord. To celebrate this meal without manifesting the total fellowship is to celebrate it in an unworthy manner, and it is a sacrilege with dire consequences. There is a warning in the fact that some are sick and some have died, and unless the Corinthians repent quickly, they will face ultimate condemnation (vv. 30-32). It is that serious.

In the history of sacramental theology this passage, and especially vv. 27-29, has played a major role. With the ever growing attention to the elements (bread and wine/body and blood), these words contributed to ever more precise speculation about real presence, transsubstantiation, etc. They have also led to closed communion–lest some would eat and drink damnation upon themselves by not having the right interpretation of the nature of the elements and the presence of the Lord. Much fear and much mutual suspicion have been engendered among and between Christians by these verses.

A careful study of 1 Cor. 11 leads us to the recapturing of the original intention, which was quite different. Paul recognized that there have to be various opinions in the church, but that is no reason for schisms (vv. 18-19; cf. chap. 3, leaving the sorting out of ultimate truth to the Lord and the last judgment; cf. 4:4-5). And at the Lord's Meal any practice that discriminates against a brother or a sister–and especially against the poor–is the sin of sins. Over against speculation about the elements, we also note how Paul follows the early tradition in always speaking about "the bread and the cup," never "the bread and the wine," an indication that his attention is on the act of the sacrament, not its elements in a (supra)naturalistic sense.

A similar link between the communion with the Lord and the unity of the community is found in the original wording of the Lord's Prayer (in Matt. 6:11-12 par.): the prayer for the bread refers to the bread of the eschatological meal, "the bread for the day that comes next" (*epiousios*). And that prayer is immediately followed by the prayer for forgiveness of what we have done wrong to our brothers and sisters and the assurance of our having forgiven those who wronged us. We note that these two prayers (for the bread of the Meal and for mutual forgiveness) are the only ones connected by an "and." Could it be more clear: The eucharist is for the whole mutually forgiven community, as Paul says in 1 Cor. 11.

Homiletical Notes to Maundy Thursday. Neither scriptures, nor sermons, meditations, or reflection can or should overshadow the central act of the Christian church this day: The eucharist placed in the setting of the night on which he was betrayed and handed over (the Greek word *paradidōmi* has both meanings) to the authorities. But our exegetical observations have indicated a far wider span of meanings and motifs than we usually associate with the Last Supper in the mood of memory. They all belong not only to Maundy Thursday, but also play into each and every celebration of the eucharist. Thus this day could be an aid toward the renewal and enrichment of the eucharistic life in our churches, in our minds and souls, in our imagination.

The word "renewal" has a special meaning when we think about the three texts before us, and we could suggest the theme: "When God makes things new." There is the *new* commandment of love that gave its name to this day. There is the Passover to which was added the *new* dimension of Jesus' broken body and spent blood, the *new* covenant. There is the looking in longing toward his coming in glory, i.e., when he will drink it *new* with us in the kingdom of his father (Matt. 26:29). There is the *new* mystery of his Body which calls forth Paul's exhortation to full sharing between all brothers and sisters, as members (*melē*, "limbs") of one another in Christ. There is the original Passover on the night when they broke away from Egypt and the unleavened bread, the symbol of *newness*, cleansed from all old leaven (cf. 1 Cor. 5:7). Both of these feasts had had their roots in the distant past of nomadic and agricultural rites, but were given *new* meaning by God's mighty acts through Moses. They became the celebration of survival and liberation, past, present, and future, sanctified by the liberation from slavery in Egypt. For what God has done once tells us what he in his own time can do again, by acts of renewal.

As the people of a new covenant in Christ with a new testament in our Bibles, we should be aware of what it means that God makes new things, or rather: makes things new.

Think about the new commandment "that you love one another" (John

13:34). As it says in 1 John 2:7, it is an old commandment, it is not new in the sense of not having been there before. The OT has it strongly, and it was one of the main points of all Jewish catechisms (cf. Matt. 22:39 par.). But it is renewed, i.e., intensified and given new weight by the new investment of God's love in Christ. The full text is: "that you love one another even as I have loved you, in order that you love one another."

And so it is with all these "new things." They are not new in the sense that inventions or ideas are new. They are old things made new. God's grace in the delivery from Egypt on the night when the first born were slaughtered, and God's grace in the sacrifice of his first born son Jesus is the same grace, as he is the same one and only God.

In our Gospel for Maundy Thursday this new intensity, this higher voltage of love is expressed in the act of the footwashing, the holy reversal of the roles of master and servants, teacher and disciples. Love is not a feeling, but a change of roles, a change of style in the life of the community. And reflecting on the oneness in the Body of Christ, Paul intensifies this understanding in his cutting remarks about the Meal in Corinth.

From him we learn that this Meal requires what he later in that letter calls love. Again, not as a feeling of warmth in the heart, but as a practical and institutionalized concern for others as they also are part of the church—however different and diverse their gifts. The sin above sins in the church, and especially at the Meal, is discrimination, racial, social, spiritual, or whatever.

On this day of the renewed Meal of divine and communal love we remember how we have distorted and tried to destroy that love. How did that happen? Often because we heard the words and tried to make the church a loving community—in our own fake manner. We thought that love was the opposite to conflicts and divided opinions. So we smiled and tried to look and feel friendly and loving in church. We wanted the feeling of love, also for P.R. purposes: For they know we are Christians by our love! We were afraid of conflict, and of those who raised difficult questions that might split the church and destroy our homemade picture of love. Or we made our community congenial enough (socially, racially, theologically) so that we could have that feeling of love undisturbed.

But Paul says that, of course, there must be differing and even conflicting opinions—as there certainly were in Corinth—but no schism. For love is measured not by feeling, but by how much tension it can stand. Paul's model of love is: The more love, the more diversity.

The message is this: When we celebrate the Meal, Christ brings us together with people whom we never would like to congregate with if we were to create our own community of love among like-minded people. The only thing that brings us together is our common participation in Christ's gift, our common need for him, our common need of sticking together in the night of deliverance and liberation.

And if it be true that even Judas was there with them, who are we to draw our lines and limits?

Good Friday

Lutheran	*Roman Catholic*	*Episcopal*	*Pres./UCC/Chr.*	*Methodist/COCU*
Isa. 52:13–53:12	Isa. 52:13–53:12	Isa. 52:13–53:12	Isa. 52:13–53:12	Isa. 52:13–53:12
Heb. 4:14–5:10	Heb. 4:14–16; 5:7–9	Heb. 10:1–25	Heb. 4:14–16; 5:7–9	Heb. 4:14–16; 5:7–9
John 18:1–19:42 (long), or John 19:17–30 (short)	John 18:1–19:42	John 18:1–19:37, or John 19:1–37	John 19:17–30	John 18:1–19:42

Gospel: John 18:1-19:42 (long); John 19:17-30 (short)—Exegesis. In our exegesis of the Matthean passion narrative we found it helpful and necessary to spell out, sometimes in some detail, many of the characteristics of the Johannine narrative, and in the exegeses of the Gospel texts for Tuesday and Maundy Thursday we have studied parts of the "bridge" between the climactic sign of the resurrection (the raising of Lazarus, chap. 11), and the events now before us. In a real sense, the farewell discourses (chaps. 14-17) are also part of John's passion. I must beg the reader to return especially to my comments on John's Gospel as it compares to that of Matthew (above, pp. 11-17) in order to get the distinct perspective of the texts now before us. And then it is time to read chapters 18 and 19 as if we had only them before us.

In such a reading we are struck by a few important things. There is no hearing or decision in the Jewish Sanhedrin or before the High Priest (Caiaphas). There is only a night interrogation with Caiaphas's father-in-law (Annas), where Jesus does not answer the questions, but refers to those who have heard his public teaching (*tō kosmō*, "to the world," 18:20). In contrast, the real encounter is with Pilate. Approximately half of these two chapters deals with that encounter. Here the two powers meet: King Jesus, whose kingdom is not of this world, and the representative of Caesar.

There is no agony in the garden, but that place (in John without a name) was known to Judas as a favorite meeting place for Jesus and his disciples. The arrest is striking. Judas's role is only to lead the troops there, now primarily Pilate's Roman troops, a whole cohort (regularly 600 men) and their commander. Jesus presents himself with the "I am" by which John always expresses Jesus' majestic proclamations and self-revelations. The troops draw back and fall to the ground.

Since Jesus is to be crucified, i.e., lifted up (cf. John 3:13, 12:32 f.; cf. above, p. 30), his execution must be at the hands of the Romans (18:31; 19:15). As in the synoptic Gospels, Pilate is pictured as unwilling to grant the request of the Jewish leaders, but he gives in. Yet by his inscription on the cross he announces the victory of Jesus: "What I have written, I have written" (19:22).

John stresses that Jesus carries his own cross, strong and unbroken (19:17). John's feeling for symbolism makes him stress that Jesus' tunic was like that of a high priest, i.e., seamless (19:24).

There are the three words from the cross of which we spoke earlier. The care for Mary his mother may be a sign of his love and concern, or it may be a special honor bestowed on the beloved disciple who is the intended author or chief witness to the gospel. Jesus then fulfills the scriptures by saying "I thirst," and his final word is the glorious word of victory (see above, p. 12). It is equally striking that John says: ". . . he handed over the spirit" (19:30). This expression differs from the synoptic Gospels. Some interpreters see it as a reference to the promised giving of the Spirit to the church (7:39; 16:7, 13; 20:23), but it is more reasonable to see it as an expression for Jesus' unbroken relationship to the Father.

There is no confession by the centurion or the guards. That is not necessary. But there is a further sign. When the soldiers come to put the three out of their misery—since the Passover is about to begin, not in order to shorten their agony—Jesus is already dead. And as a soldier pierces his chest with a lance, blood and water flow. Interpreters have given medical explanations of this phenomenon. Some have even argued that this "surgery" plus the coolness of the tomb account for his resuscitation a short time later. But such speculations are singularly misplaced, especially in the Gospel of John. To him the meaning is symbolic: The sacraments of baptism and the eucharist are alluded to (cf. 3:5; 7:38 f.; 6:53-57; also 1 John 5:8). This final sign is of great importance to John; hence the stress on the beloved apostle—as the eyewitness. By this final sign Jesus became the passover lamb on which "you shall break no bone" (Gen. 12:46), and as he has been "lifted up" above the earth they will look upon him whom they have pierced (Zech. 12:10; cf. Rev. 1:7).

Nicodemus now joins Joseph of Arimathea at the grave. The two who had been disciples in secret venture forth in an act of love. Jesus' grave is new and unused.

The majestic death of Jesus according to the Gospel of John reminds us of earlier Christian art. Long before there were crucifixes with the suffering Jesus, plagued by the crown of thorns, the Jesus of Bernard of Clairvaux and Paul Gerhardt (O Sacred Head Now Wounded), there was the triumphal crucifix with the victorious Jesus standing in royal and priestly garb, hands outstretched in the blessing embrace of the world. Actually, the crown of thorns of which all the Gospels speak was presumably not a torturesome crown, but the long thorns were placed like the sunrays surrounding the royal head on imperial coins (and on the Statue of Liberty). It was a mocking crown which in God's irony was the true crown of glory. "What I have written, I have written!", as Pilate said.

When faith narrates and gives its loving witness in the Gospel of John, it tries to tell us of a power and a glory that are not of this world; therefore—we should not say "and yet"—it is *the* power and *the* glory.

This is a glorious death, but it is not a death in human heroism. How can there be "heroism" when he knows at all times the glorious outcome? It is the mysterious death of God's own Son. There are no signs of unusual human courage or bravery, nor is there the slightest suggestion that people like you and me should emulate this death of Jesus. No, this is the glorification, the exaltation of God's Son. It is all of another order of magnitude than anything known to human experience. The response can only be—already at the cross—that of Thomas: "My Lord and my God!" For that is, after all, the response toward which this whole gospel was written (John 20:28-31).

First Lesson: Isa. 52:14-53:12—Exegesis. It is impossible for a Christian—or anyone who reads the passion narratives—not to think about Jesus as the Suffering Servant of Yahweh in this the fourth of the Servant songs. We are reminded of the story of how Philip answered the question of the Ethiopian eunuch who was reading Isa. 53:7 and asked: "About whom does the prophet speak? About himself or about someone else?" And Philip "took this passage as his text as he brought him the gospel of Jesus" (Acts 8:32-35; cf. perhaps Luke 24:26).

In the light of our feeling of a close relation between Isa. 53 and the Passion of Jesus it is surprising how few specific references there are in the NT to this song, and some of them do not even relate to the saving death of Jesus. Matthew's only quotation refers to Jesus' healing ministry (8:17); John 12:38 and Rom. 10:16 speak about lack of faith in general; and in Rom. 15:21 the quotation from the song substantiates Paul's missionary principle of visiting only places where the gospel has not yet been preached. Specific passion references to Isa. 53 are found in passages where the texts are uncertain and possibly later additions (Luke 23:34; Mark 15:28; cf., however, Luke 22:37). The most extensive quotation from Isa. 53 is in the climax of an exhortation to submissiveness of servants to their masters, 1 Peter 2:21-25, i.e., an appeal to the moral example (v. 21) of Christ (cf. Phil. 2, the Second Lesson for Passion Sunday, and also Mark 10:45 par.). The Passion narratives themselves seem to have been shaped more by Psalms 22 and 69, and the deeply suggestive fourth song of the Servant did not enter Christian reflection on the Passion until later.

The text of the song is difficult at many points, and already Jewish translations (as the Greek Septuagint) and interpretations have left their marks in the manuscripts, as have Christian emendations. The classical question remains that of the Ethiopian eunuch: Who is this Servant? Is it the prophet himself, perhaps as seen by his devout followers? Is it Israel as she carries out her mission among the nations? Is it the true Israel, the remnant purified by suffering? Is it the expected Messiah, or at least a messianic figure of the future? Is it a timeless personification of meaningful and redemptive suffering, seen as a critique of popular wisdom's idea that suffering is a sign of God's disfavor? Is it thus an elaboration of the figure of Job, seen in the light of martyrdom?

Scholars and Bible readers, ancient and modern, have tried out all these possibilities and more, and we are tempted to say that all these interpretations see something that actually is there. As a true poem, it does not lend itself to narrow definitions of meaning. Perhaps we do best by just listening to the next. For the main theme is very clear.

The Servant is afflicted and disfigured. Thus people think that he is smitten by God, and in accordance with Near Eastern understanding, it was dangerous to look at one who was an obvious object of divine anger. He was "as one from whom people hide their faces." The nature of his affliction is of many kinds, and the poet is not interested in the specifics but in the total effect: he was afflicted in all ways. He even died, by perverted and oppressive judgment, and his grave was with the wicked and the rich (which is the same thing here, as in Luke, e.g., 16:25; only in Matthew is Joseph of Arimathea "rich," 27:57).

But the Servant bore all this affliction according to the will of God; it was our ills, and sorrows, and pain, and transgressions, and iniquities that he bore. "Yahweh brought the transgressions of all of us to meet upon him" (v. 6, the Anchor Bible's translation). Thus he became—he even gave himself as—an atoning guilt offering. In vv. 10-12, where Yahweh is again the speaker (as in 52:13-15), it is affirmed that the Servant will be vindicated and thereby also the plan of Yahweh, "the will of the Lord," toward the restoration of those for whom the Servant bore the sin and made intercession.

This powerful and deeply moving poem certainly applies to many situations. It certainly applies to the suffering history of Israel and her mission among the nations (cf. the earlier Songs, with their global outreach, see above Sunday through Tuesday). It certainly applies to martyrs and prophets through the ages. It certainly applies to the Passion of Jesus in the faith of the church. Although there is no clear indication thereof, the Song may even have sustained him in his week of agony. And the intention of the Song was just that: A mighty song for the sustaining of those who suffer innocently.

Second Lesson: Heb. 4:14-5:10—Exegesis. The Epistle to the Hebrews sees Jesus Christ against the full background of Israel's history

(1:1-4; cf. Acts 7, and also above, the Second Lesson for Monday). That the Son is greater than the angels is demonstrated by a series of quotations (1:5–2:18). When the author comes to Ps. 8:7, he reads "You made him *for a little while* [Hebrew and Greek OT: "a little"] lower than the angels" and reflects on the manner in which Jesus' tasting death made him one with the human condition and thus Jesus was not ashamed to call us "brothers" (2:8-13). Jesus' likeness with us humans had to be, in order to make him the right merciful high priest, offering expiation for the people, a high priest capable of helping those put to the test, since he himself had suffered much testing (2:17-18).

It is this theme that is taken up again in our passage, after a meditation on the temptations and trials in the wilderness on the way to the "sabbath rest in Canaan." That "rest" is now promised anew in Jesus, the second Joshua (4:8; in Greek both names are written "Jesus"). But only those who hold fast will enter, and God's word exposes the truth about us (4:12-14).

Yet, we have a merciful high priest and thus we can approach God's throne, since Jesus is now enthroned next to God (8:1; 12:2; cf. 1:8), having transcended the heavenly spheres. The reason for his mercy is specific. He understands, since he has experienced our trials, and the fact that he did so without sin does not place him in a different category or nature.

The KJV and the RSV speak of "temptation," while the NEB translates "test" (cf. the Lord's prayer in the new liturgies: "Do not put us to the test"). The Greek word is the same (*peirasmos*), and means trial-test-temptation. The choice is up to the interpreter and the context. I would think that the author of Hebrews does not think of general temptations, but of the specific tests of martyrdom and the risk of apostasy (cf. 6:6; 12:4). Thus the approach to the throne is not the scene of the last judgment, but the seeking of help "in time" (4:16) when undergoing trials and tribulations. That interpretation is supported by the image of Jesus and his prayers, obviously a reference to Gethsemane and the cross. The trial is suffering, and it is in martyrdom that obedience is learned and the trust in God is tested.

Hebrews brings in the analogy of the Aaronic high priests. They can deal gently with the ignorant and the erring since they have to offer sacrifices for themselves as well as for the people. Jesus learned this gentleness through his human suffering, but his sacrifice is more powerful since he did not need to offer it for himself. That line of thought is interrupted by another: All high priests are called by God, and so was Jesus according to the continuation of the favorite christological Psalm 110 (quoted in Heb. 1:3, 13; 8:1) where the fourth verse declares: "You are a priest forever according to the order of Melchizedek" (cf. 9:11-16, above Monday).

In Hebrews Jesus Christ is truly exalted. He is higher than the angels, enthroned, and a high priest forever; note the word "perfected" (*teleiōtheis*, v. 9), a key word in Hebrews, referring to the ultimate and heavenly realm (cf. John 19:30, *tetelestai*). But his passion is a real passion. It is the source of his compassion for those who need help in time of trial and tribulation. There may be worse tests to come. Then they must look to Jesus, the pioneer and perfecter of their faith (chap. 12). That is how they will find help in time.

Good Friday—Homiletical Notes. In the English speaking world this day is known as Good Friday. When you come to think about it, that is a strange designation. The day of the death of Jesus, still only in his thirties, the day when his beautiful life came to an end, when he was betrayed and deserted and ridiculed and manhandled, the day when the acts of powerful people culminated in the shame of a crucifixion—how can we call that day good? In other Christian countries they do not call it so. In Sweden, for example, they call it the Long Friday. That term expresses the identification with his pain and shame, and the long hours on the cross, and it suggests how the day was kept distinct and holy as all activities stopped and the mood of mourning dominated the day, the one day of the year when not only shops, but restaurants and theaters were closed.

But in calling the day Good Friday, we look rather at the results, the fruits, the consequences of his death. The Johannine Gospel and its passion narrative is the right text for the understanding of this day as good. The Passion is not geared toward a pilgrimage along the *via dolorosa*, where we would identify in our sinfulness with the various actors in the drama, or where we would be stirred in our sympathy for the man of sorrows as if he were a tragic hero. To be sure he does not need our sympathy or our tears. Nor are we invited to imitate his humility and obedience.

Our imitation would be arrogant, for we are not primarily followers, we are the beneficiaries, the heirs, the recipients of his mighty glorification on the cross.

> Now above the Cross, the trophy,
> Sound the loud triumphant lay:
> Tell how Christ, the world's Redeemer,
> As a Victim won the day.
> (SBH 61, one of the oldest passion hymns, from the 6th century)

There is no good English word for the German *Andacht* or the Swedish word *betraktelse.* They both express an attitude of quiet, silent looking at the picture painted before our eyes by the scriptures. Such a meditation is what this day calls for. We are invited to see, and the response almost has to be in song and poetry. To attach moral lessons would be self-centered and rash or premature.

For here the death of Christ is seen from God's perspective, not from that of the bystanders or even the followers. As John often refers to the relationship between the Father and the Son, so he has tried to tell of Good Friday as from within the heart and mind of God. What is seen and heard by the faithful witness, the beloved disciple, is how the benefits of this death flow from the side of Christ, blood and water, the sacramental power in the sustaining eucharist and in the baptism of rebirth from above.

This is the victory of God, not in spite of death, but by and through a transfigured death. "For as the Father has life in himself, so he has granted the Son also to have life in himself" (John 5:26).

His death is not our death, but through his mysterious death a new power of life flows into the world. The cross has become the tree of life.

> Faithful Cross; above all other
> One and only noble Tree!
> None in foliage, none in blossom
> None in fruit thy peer may be;
> Sweetest wood and sweetest iron;
> Sweetest weight is hung on thee.
>
> (SBH 61, v. 3)

God so loved the world that the Friday on which his Son died by human hands became the Good Friday.

Also the Servant (Isa. 53) is an awesome manifestation of that mystery. The vindication is sure. In God's hands his martyrdom becomes a graceful sacrifice for those who did not understand, but for whom he offered intercession.

The Second Lesson of Good Friday interprets that sacrifice, and in doing so it presents the inverted image of the *imitatio Christi*. For it is not we who are urged to imitate Christ, but God sent his Son to learn the *imitatio hominum*, the imitation and identification with the human condition. In his suffering he became our brother, lest we be blinded by his glory or discouraged to the point of despair.

[For the Seven Words Spoken from the Cross, see above, pp. 11-12, and 48].

Appendix: The Gospel of Peter

Since I have found it helpful, clarifying, enlightening, and stimulating in our study of the Holy Week texts to refer to the Gospel of Peter from time to time, I am offering here this translation of it—which I have made rather literal in order to retain the flavor of the Greek as much as possible. This fragment, found in Egypt in the winter of 1886-87, is all that survives of the apocryphal Gospel of Peter, a second century document known to the church fathers. For an introduction, bibliography, and a somewhat different translation—in which the echo from the canonical Gospels is made stronger than it is in the actual Greek text of the Gospel of Peter—see E. Hennecke—W. Schneemelcher (eds.), *New Testament Apocrypha, vol. 1: Gospels and Related Writings.* (Philadelphia: Westminster, 1963). The section on the Gospel of Peter (pp. 179-87), including translation, is by Chr. Maurer and was translated into English by George Ogg.

THE GOSPEL OF PETER

1 . . . but none of the Jews washed the hands, neither Herod nor any member of his court; and as they did not want to wash, Pilate arose.

2 And then King Herod gives the order that the Lord be taken away, saying to them: "Carry out what I have ordered you to do to him!" 3 But there stood Joseph, the friend of Pilate and of the Lord, and knowing that they were about

to crucify him, he went to Pilate and asked for the body of the Lord for burial. 4 And Pilate sent to Herod the request for his body, 5 and Herod said: "Brother Pilate, even if someone had not asked for him, we would have buried him since the Sabbath is approaching. For it is written in the Law 'The sun may not set upon someone executed.' " And he handed him over to the people on the day before the Unleavened Bread, their feast.

6 But as they took hold of the Lord they pushed him, all running, and they said: "Let us drag the Son of God with us as we have got him in our power." 7 And they dressed him in purple and placed him on the judicial bench and said: "Judge right, O king of Israel." 8 And one of them brought a thorn crown and placed it on the head of the Lord, 9 and other bystanders spat him in the face, or hit his cheeks, or pricked him with a reed; and some scourged him, saying: "Let us honor the Son of God with this honor!"

10 And they brought two criminals and they crucified the Lord between them, but he remained silent as one having no pain. 11 And when they had raised up the cross they wrote on it: "This is the king of Israel." 12 And they laid out his clothes before him and divided them and cast lot about them. 13 But one of those criminals rebuked them, saying: "We have suffered in this manner because of the evil we did, but this man has become the savior of mankind, what wrong has he done to you?" 14 And they got angry with him and ordered that his legs not be broken so that he might die fully tortured.

15 Now it was noontime and darkness came over the whole of Judea and they became worried and afraid that the sun had set already, for he was still alive. For it is written for them: "The sun may not set upon someone executed." 16 And one of them said: "Give him gall with sour wine to drink." And they mixed it and gave him to drink, 17 and fulfilled everything and completed the sins upon their heads. 18 And many went around with lamps in the thought that night had come. 19 Then the Lord cried out: "My Power, my Power, you have left me!" Having said so, he was taken up. 20 And in the same hour the veil of the Temple of Jerusalem was split in two.

21 And then they pulled the spikes out of the hands of the Lord and laid him on the earth. And the whole earth shook and there was great fear. 22 Then the sun broke through and it was found to be 3 pm, 23 and the Jews were happily relieved and his body they gave to Joseph so that he would bury it since he had seen all the good he had done. 24 And he took the Lord, washed him and wrapped him in a linen shroud, and brought him into his own tomb, called the Garden of Joseph.

25 Then the Jews and the elders and the priests—aware of how great evil they had done to themselves—went into lament and said: "Woe upon our sins! The judgment and the end of Jerusalem have come close!" 26 But I—with my friends—was in sorrow, and with wounded hearts we hid ourselves, for they were now after us as after criminals and people intending to burn down the Temple. 27 But in all this we were fasting and sat mourning and weeping night and day until the Sabbath.

28 But the theologians and the pharisees and the elders met together. They were told that all the people complained and beat their breasts in contrition, saying: "If by his death these the greatest signs have happened, see how righteous he is." 29 Thus the elders got afraid and came to Pilate with this request:

30 "Supply us with soldiers in order that they guard his tomb for three days,
lest his disciples steal him and the people surmise that he arose, and they do
us harm." 31 And Pilate supplied them with the centurion Petronius and sol-
diers to guard the tomb, and the elders and the theologians came with them to
the tomb, 32 and all who were there, together with the centurion and the sol-
diers, placed a great stone over the entrance of the tomb rolling and tilting it,
33 sealed it with seven seals, pitched tent there, and kept watch. 34 And early
at dawn on the Sabbath a crowd from Jerusalem and its surroundings came to
see the sealed tomb.

35 But in the night when the Lord's day dawned, while the soldiers kept
watch, two in each shift, there was a great sound in heaven, 36 and they saw
the heavens opened and two men descended from there in much brightness
and standing at the tomb. 37 And that stone placed against the tomb began to
roll by itself and moved to one side, and the tomb opened and the young men
both entered. 38 When now those soldiers saw this, they awakened the cen-
turion and the elders, for they were also there as part of the watch. 39 And as
they tell what they had seen, they see three men coming out from the tomb,
the two supporting the one, and a cross following them, 40 and the head of the
two reaching to heaven, but that of the one whom they led reaching beyond
the heavens, 41 and they heard a voice from the heavens: "You have preached
to those who sleep!" 42 and an answer was heard from the cross, giving the
"Yes!"

43 Then those men deliberated about going and informing Pilate about this.
44 And while they still are deliberating, the heavens are again seen opened and
a person having descended and entered into the tomb. 45 When the centurion's
men saw that, they rushed to Pilate, leaving the tomb they were guarding, and
told, highly upset, all that they had seen, and they said: "He was truly the
Son of God." 46 Pilate answered: "I am clean of the blood of the Son of God;
this was your decision." 47 Then they all came to him and pleaded with him,
beseeching him to order the centurion and the soldiers to tell nobody what
they had seen. 48 "It is better," they said, "for us to become guilty of the great-
est sin before God, than to fall into the hands of the Jewish people and be
stoned." 49 So Pilate ordered the centurion and the soldiers to tell nothing.

50–51 In the early morning of the Lord's day Mary Magdalene, a disciple of
the Lord, took with her her women friends and came to the tomb where he
was laid—for out of fear for the Jews, since they were inflamed with anger, she
had not done to the tomb of the Lord what women are expected to do to their
loved ones when they die. 52 And they were afraid lest the Jews would see
them, and they said: "Even if we could not weep and lament on that day when
he was crucified, so let us do so now at his tomb. 53 But who is to roll away
for us that stone placed against the entrance of the tomb, so that we can go in
and sit with him and do what is due? 54 For the stone was great and we are
afraid, lest somebody sees us. And if we cannot, let us place at the door what
we are bringing to his memorial. We shall weep and lament until we have ar-
rived back home." 55 And they went along and found the tomb opened, and
they approached and stooped down there, and they see there a certain young
man seated in the center of the tomb, beautiful and dressed in a brightly shin-
ing robe. He said to them: 56 "Why have you come? Whom are you looking

for? Not the one who was crucified? He arose and left. But if you do not be-
lieve, stoop down and see the place where he lay, that he is not there. For he
arose and left for the place from which he was sent." 57 Then the women fled
in fear. 58 But it was the final day of (the feast of) Unleavened Bread and
many left and returned to their homes, the feast being over. 59 But we, the
twelve disciples of the Lord, wept and mourned, and each went to his home,
grieved by the events.

60 But I Simon Peter and my brother Andrew took our nets and went to the
sea, and with us was Levi, the son of Alpheus, whom the Lord . . .